The Participant Principle

A guide to getting the best recruitment for your user testing and qualitative research

Maya Middlemiss is the Managing Director of *Saros Research* in the UK and *Casslar Consulting SL* in Spain.

Saros Research is the UK's leading database-driven market research and user experience participant recruitment company, recruiting participants for a diverse range of qualitative, social and technical projects across all consumer and B2B market sectors.

Maya describes herself as a proactive and progressive project manager, with a fantastic team at Saros, passionate about excellence in customer service and project delivery. Her extensive market research fieldwork experience, combined with a background in community development and diversity, allow her to offer expert consultancy on any research recruitment project from social to user experience and technology. This 'can-do' attitude and alignment with clients' values and objectives extends throughout the Saros organisation.

Through *Casslar Consulting*, Maya is a Consultant and speaker on social media, marketing and entrepreneurship, she is a columnist for *Costa News* and author of http://costaconnected.com. Maya also blogs about business, social media, location independence and other topics. She is a Certified Member of the Market Research Society, and an Individual Member of ESOMAR and the Association for Qualitative Research.

First published in Great Britain in 2016 by U P Publications Ltd
Eco Innovation Centre PetersCourt, City Road Peterborough UK

Cover concept © 2016 Maya Middlemiss and U P Publications

A CIP Catalogue record of this book is available
from the British Library

Paperback ISBN 978-1-908135-73-5

eBook ISBN 978-1-908135-74-2

FIRST PAPERBACK EDITION

7 1 0 2 9 3 4 8 5 6

Published by U P Publications
Printed in England by The Lightning Source Group

www.uppbooks.com
www.sarosresearch.com

The
Participant Principle

A guide to getting the best
recruitment for your user testing
and qualitative research

Maya Middlemiss

U P Publications Ltd
2016

Contents

Foreword

"Be a yardstick for quality. Some people aren't used to an environment where excellence is expected."

Steve Jobs

In the quest to create an excellent meal, ingredients are critical: high quality, great balance, tastes and textures come together to transport and inspire each and every one at the table. Combined with the chef's imagination, passion, flair, commitment and diligence, the experience can be outstanding.

The same fundamentals apply to great insight work: the higher the quality of ingredients, the greater the chance of creating something outstanding.

This book is a hands-on approach to the delivery of excellence in recruitment. Recruitment is so fundamental to what we do, and is often fraught with challenge and risk. Not only can it be difficult to simply get it right and on specification, but there is every chance something will go wrong on the night.

This book helps us all understand what we can do to mitigate the risk and maximise the potential for a powerful learning and inspirational experience for practitioners and clients. It gives useful direction as to how to navigate the

muddy waters and come out with a clear result. It distils many years of experience and ongoing innovation into simple and easy to read guidelines, and sets out the fundamentals for success in a modern, digital world.
Enjoy!

Katie Oakley
Founding Partner, MEAT

The Participant Principle

Why Do Participants Matter So Much?

At Saros, we know your research participants are the fundamental raw materials, for whatever you intend to accomplish in your research.

Whatever techniques and insight you bring to bear to solve your client's problem will only be effective if applied to the right qualitative input, and the participants are the foundation on which you will build your report.

As Katie Oakley says, when baking a cake, it is the skill of the baker in choosing and using the right recipe with the correct ingredients that dictates the final taste. What marks a great baker is the experience, insight and unique personal twist that is brought to the process to produce a perfect balance of flavour and presentation.

While a standard recipe might accomplish something palatable – if the ingredients are of inferior quality, or simply wrong, then the finished product will not stand the taste test.

If, between us, we can get these vital ingredients right however, it all comes together on the plate. Your insight generation gets built on the right foundations. Your participants will inform hypotheses, embody personas, indicate strategic direction, and give you and your client what you need – the confidence to take decisions that can be relied upon, and get results.

Of course, individual participants might challenge or contradict each other or, indeed, your stimulus – because they're confident about their terms of engagement and not afraid to disagree and to explain why. However, if the recruitment has been procured and managed effectively that 'why' will be a valid finding in itself, because they are the right target and you can learn from them, in precise terms, how and why the results differ from what may have been expected.

If you have confidence in your participants and, by extension, in the process that delivered them, you can be confident exploring these divergences – instead of dismissing them as an outlier or error. These are the kind of sessions that create genuine serendipity and potential for pivots and shifts, even new products and services. We love it when a researcher feeds back to us that their client keeps talking about one golden idea which emerged from the group, that may not even relate to the discussion guide, but which, somehow, sparks something genuinely fresh and new for them.

Good recruitment also means consistency. You know that you have the right people in the room and can do your best work, even if your client's entire creative department is behind the mirror (or watching live-streamed). We know that clients don't always agree with one another, that there can be conflicting agendas in play or different interests in the outcome of the qualitative exercise. We know it's essential that you have confidence in your recruitment, so that you can manage your clients' expectations with credibility, whilst staying focussed on their objectives on the night. It means that all the participants arriving are prepared for what will happen, are a spot-on match with your spec and have something interesting to say too – lots of great verbatims for your report and creative ideas you can reflect and expand upon, to generate actionable insight for your client.

As a professional, you can, of course, do a lot with any respondent who simply checks the right boxes, but we appreciate that so much more can be done with a participant who has real enthusiasm and creativity where it's needed, the right background towards the project in terms of attitude and behavioural profile and who brings their own imagination to bear on the ideas generation process.

However, it has often seemed to us (and to the researchers we consult), that the recruitment process is something clients rarely consider, and sometimes overlook or simply fail to prioritise during the earliest stages of project planning. Developing a recruitment specification and working effectively with recruitment agencies may be something in which junior researchers receive little formal training. Alongside all the other skills they have to acquire and apply, expectations and reality may have become out of alignment by the time the recruitment is ready to brief out.

We are passionate about participants, because we know how important they are. We want the researchers we work with to get the best possible people to work with, those who will put the greatest efforts into their contributions. This guide will help you to get the most out of the recruitment services you commission for every research project you do.

Participant Recruitment has Evolved

For many decades, recruitment in the UK proceeded largely unchanging, as a cottage-industry network of individuals. Recruiters, who often hosted research in their own homes, had extensive address books and contacts and, in the best cases worked door-to-door to find appropriate participants.

They were co-ordinated by supervisors, also largely freelance, who contracted in turn to larger fieldwork agencies.

Nowadays, participant recruitment increasingly takes place online, reaching far greater networks and numbers than ever before, leading to an explosion of providers. These providers are needed, as larger numbers of people are researching directly with members of the public (on and off line) than ever before, needing more and more participants. This has had mixed effects on the industry as a whole.

A further change which has had a significant impact on the recruitment industry is that not every researcher has had the typical career path of the traditional research executive. A decade or so back, most of the researchers we worked directly with were either senior and had many years of experience in their craft, or they were working as a junior in a team, delivering agency-side projects for external clients.

Nowadays, there are tools available for people to design, create and test their own products easily in small companies and many more businesses have their own research centres in-house.

Increasingly, people are looking at ways to gain

consumer insight faster and more cost-effectively.

As recruiters, we aren't here to comment on what that means for the quality of the research produced by such methods, but it has created a market in which professional skills in recruitment are more and more necessary - if only to ensure that fieldwork adheres to industry standards and protects the wellbeing and reputation of all parties.

If anything goes wrong during fieldwork – if a single participant has a negative experience for whatever reason – then that reflects on our whole industry.

People are more likely to talk about negative events than positive ones, and they can now talk to more people more quickly than ever before. This doesn't happen often, but it's important to bear in mind that the effects of non-researchers doing research, on and offline, muddies the waters that define our craft - and this can impact negatively on perceptions and reputation.

We are committed to the professionalisation of research participant recruitment, particularly for qualitative research, which works at such a different level to quantitative surveys. The way qualitative processes get participants to reflect and articulate their non-conscious beliefs and attitudes and provide reasons for behaviour, makes those participants intrinsically more vulnerable as a result, however mundane the subject matter might be.

We have an absolute responsibility to ensure that they are recruited and managed completely ethically and responsibly. The business case for this is very clear – happy participants, who have a positive experience taking part in research, will spread the word, encouraging more and more potential participants in future.

The New Participants

The most important effect-change that online communications have brought about is the widening access to research participation and the removal of the gatekeepers (in the form of the traditional recruiters' network). This is very exciting, both for researchers and potential participants, because it means that fundamental restrictions are at least partially removed.

The difficulty with the traditional recruiters' network is partly that it is demographically unrepresentative, consisting largely of women, in specific age, class and ethnicity categories.

Whilst many traditional recruiters are very well networked – including some truly phenomenal Gladwellian connectors – there are practical limits to how many individuals anyone can really remember or stay in touch with. Inevitably, we will tend to know more people who are in some way similar to ourselves, than we know people who are totally different. That's simple human nature, nothing sinister, we all associate with those with whom we share something in common. It only becomes inappropriate when a particular demographic is a barrier to access within an industry acting as a portal to public opinion.

As such, until quite recently, many researchers complained that they tended to see, if not the same faces repeatedly in research (which is a different problem), then certainly the same *kinds* of faces. We have had researchers tell us they have rarely seen a non-white face in fieldwork, that they have never knowingly seen a disabled person. I have had researchers tell me that none of their friends or people they meet has ever heard of the *idea* of taking part in paid research exercises, they've not known how to proceed or find out about it. They've told us they would actually love to see people like their friends in their groups, rather than the people they were actually sent...

The flip-side of this, of course, is that consistently and for years many potentially excellent participants were excluded from taking part, without even knowing about it. This is not only unfair, it's bad for research, and for the strategic decision-making it informs.

Today's database-driven approaches have significantly levelled the playing field. It needs further levelling and this is something we are actively working on – including improving accessibility of our content and screening tools.

Widening access to research participation by using the technology available, means more people than ever before can have the opportunity to take part in research – earning incentives, as well as directly influencing the brands and services they need.

For researchers it means that, with the right approach and a realistic expectation, they can get what they need and deserve – the right people, ready to make the right contributions to their project. It doesn't depend on whether they are personally known to a tight network of individual recruiters, or whether they are in a traditional area for research, where recruiters happen to live. If they are out there and can be motivated effectively to become participants, then they can be recruited. The challenge and skill lies in finding them, within a meaningful timeframe and budget to fit most research jobs; finding a way of presenting the opportunity to them, in an attractive and compelling way, because not every participant is driven by the cash incentive.

When these two things are done, the new research participant becomes just about anyone – the recruiter's art lies in making that connection, with the right participant, at the right time, in the right way.

Rights of Participants and the Market Research Society Code of Conduct

Because qualitative research and user testing involves working directly with members of the public, there are codes of ethics in place within which this contact must take place. In the UK, the code of conduct applied is that of the Market Research Society. All recruiters should work within this framework. In other markets, the codes provided by ESOMAR, or other regional bodies, may take priority – but they all start from a similar bedrock of principles, designed to protect all parties and preserve the integrity of the research exercise itself.

These codes incorporate interpretations of current data protection legislation, such as, in the UK, the 1998 data protection act and subsequent amendments. The most up-to-date version of the MRS code can always be found at **www.mrs.org.uk/standards/code_of_conduct** along with detailed interpretive guidance, and all ESOMAR codes can be found at **http://goo.gl/BUBI69**

Some elements of the code are concerned with how the research is conducted and reported in transparent and honest ways, but a number of elements contain specific guidance about how to work with members of the public, when they take part in quantitative or qualitative research.

One of the most important of these relates to **voluntary informed consent** – this reflects the right of participants to understand exactly what they are getting involved in when they take part in research. The purpose of the exercise needs to be made clear, so far as it affects them, and they need to understand what will be done with any information or responses they provide. People can only give consent to activities they understand – so they deserve a clear and appropriate explanation of the scope of the exercise before they commit to it, what activities it will involve them in, and the fact that, if they choose to do so, they have a right to withdraw from this at any point. It means that participation in research must always be transparent about what it is, research information cannot be gleaned from other activities, which would mean that people did not know what it was they were involved with, or that was pretending to be something different.

Other important areas of the code relate to **confidentiality** and anonymity. These are actually separate concepts, because the quality of research itself depends upon the participants feeling safe enough to share information freely, without reservation, throughout the process.

Within qualitative research that takes place in groups, most often first names only are used within the group, to ensure this. Participants are not identified by name in any analysis or reporting, but confidentiality may well go beyond anonymity, and require additional steps to be taken to protect the identity of participants. If video clips are used in reportage, or if the participant pool itself is less anonymous to start with, such as research about employee satisfaction taking place within the organisation, it is essential that specific views expressed cannot be traced back to the individuals who made them.

Participant confusion can of course arise when recruited for market research they are assured is confidential, only to find that we request detailed contact information from them, not to mention the extensive profiling information we hold about them on our database.

Of course, we require that contact information to ensure good administration of the project itself, to be certain we have multiple ways to contact them. There might also be elements of screening involved. However, we must ensure that this data is separated from their identifying details before it is presented, or passed on, to any client and we must remember our responsibilities to explain this separation clearly.

In fact, this separation of the opinions and feedback from the identity of the person providing it, is the fundamental distinction of market research from any other data collection exercise – such as direct marketing or promotions. It is one of the most straightforward ways to identify such exercises being bogusly passed off as research when they are not. The Market Research Society and other bodies fight to stop terms like 'survey' being wielded by marketing database compilers and other non-researchers, who do not separate identifying from behavioural data in this way.

The Code also clarifies that market research must be clearly separated from any marketing or sales activity.

This can be confusing for participants. The word 'market' is contained within it, the content often refers directly to brands, and of course the insights generated from research participation in the commercial sector are generally understood to be intended to sell more stuff in the long run… But, during the research itself, absolutely no marketing, canvassing, or any other related actions must occur. This includes making gifts or incentive payments of clients' products (please see 'avoiding Sugging').

The **well-being of participants** is also fundamental. Nobody must be harmed or left worse off – in a material, emotional or any other sense – as a result of being involved in market research. This sounds obvious but the interpretation can be complex, and has much greater significance for qualitative research, than for those filling in a quick survey. For example, it is possible that during research about sensitive, social policy issues, there may be discussion of incidents that trigger upsetting incidents for participants, or they may learn something negative about products they are loyal to. It is important that all discussion guides and recruitment procedures are designed with the holistic welfare of participants in mind, because participants *"must not be harmed or adversely affected"* by their involvement.

This also means that they must not feel deceived or misled at any point – which can have implications for the practice of 'blind recruitment', where we specifically obscure the client's brand for reasons of robust screening and lack of priming. Our solution to this is to be completely transparent with participants who ask, and explain that *yes,* the research is on behalf of one of the brands in the list we are asking them about, and which one this is, will become apparent at some point during the research exercise itself – but it is not our place to reveal it. We might not always know ourselves, as the recruiters, and we don't want to influence their responses. We may also ask about negative feelings or experiences with brands if this is likely to have any effect on their ability to participate safely, and effectively, in the research.

As part of ensuring this well-being, the code also makes it clear that research must be conducted by people who are appropriately trained and skilled in the work they will be carrying out. There can, in truth, be difficulties for us as a supplier, to determine this fact in advance. Whilst our own business terms require that all activities we recruit for are conducted under the auspices of the Code, we cannot directly enquire as to the CVs of everybody we work for, and have to trust our instincts and experience to identify when anything might not be going as it should. We can no longer assume that every brief we get is being supervised by a trained and experienced research executive, and our sole focus has to be for the welfare of those we recruit to take part.

In the event that participants are recruited for a purpose that goes beyond the MRS code, and is an activity that is not purely market research, then this must be made absolutely explicit at the outset. (See "recruiting hybrid research projects").

The Role of the Recruiter, the Traditional Scapegoat?

It's fair to say that, amongst researchers, participant recruiters often have a less-than professional reputation. We understand the reasons for this, and it's true that standards within the industry remain highly variable

It is inevitable that if two or more veteran qualitative researchers get together socially, particularly in the presence of alcoholic beverages, then stories from the trenches abound. War stories from those whose experiences date back to the heyday of in-home group recruitment – tales of stale sandwiches, smelly dogs, disruptive children... Disasters always make the best and most memorable anecdotes, but it's clear that the innate curiosity and sense of adventure of the born 'quallie' gets tested to the limit, when engaging directly with participants on their own turf.

We salute the courage and tenacity of those who research at the front line, having ethnographic encounters with complete strangers, engaging in deep conversations about any particular aspect of their consumer behaviour, sometimes for hours at a time.

At its best, of course, this is where the most wonderful

moments occur, and the greatest insight generated, but a lot of factors have to be right for the right insights to be brought into being, and working with the right participants in the first place is absolutely essential.

So we are not at all surprised at researchers being happy to share their own horror stories of fieldwork that went cringingly or hilariously wrong, or participants that were not as expected. Recruitment tends to get the blame for this – sometimes quite justifiably, if work has been done poorly or even, in some cases, dishonestly. Participants who are mis-recruited, caught out in lies, or just plainly inappropriate in some other way, make for excruciating or sometimes simply impossible sessions, in addition to wasting huge amounts of time and money.

We would respond that whilst there is, of course, malpractice amongst a small number of providers, there are always risks when working with members of the public in all their weird wonderfulness. At times, inadequate briefing causes problems, by overlooking vital things that should have been in the screener. There might be problems with non-existent samples, or issues beyond anyone's control, such as transport crises.

Sometimes the problems are easy to pinpoint. At other times they might be complex and layered. The traditional approach, using a complex network of different suppliers relaying to one another in turn, meant that there were lots of stages along the pathway where mistakes or assumptions could become incorporated into the understanding of what was required.

Of course, if it all goes wrong on the night and you have a furious and upset client on your hands, one easy way out can be to blame the recruitment. We have known this happen on occasion – to the embarrassment of the researcher – when a perfectly on-spec group simply hated the creative output that they were testing, being viewed by the people who had developed it … But 'bad recruitment' can also be a lazy excuse for something else going wrong or for an unwanted research finding, and we maintain that it should not be the default response.

The difficulty is, that countless researchers we worked with in the past, have encountered not just low professional standards, but have actually experienced outright lies and deceit. Not just with respondents being other than who they are supposed to be, but with the recruiters who briefed them on how to perform, colluding in what amounts to fraud in the extreme.

Judging the participant recruitment industry by the behaviour of the worst examples does nothing to raise standards or improve things for the whole industry, and we have been striving for fifteen years to improve the professionalism of our service, working in genuine partnership with quality-driven researchers.

We know from the feedback we receive that recruitment really matters, and can make all the difference.

Recruiters Represent Researchers

Researchers who treat their recruiters with lack of professional respect, or who opt to work with providers they do not regard as professional equals, don't always appreciate one important implication of this. It's something that goes beyond the viewing facility in every sense.

Recruiters are the 'public face' of the research industry. We represent the work done, both to the participants and to the world at large – including all those people who haven't yet taken part in research and don't even know how much they would enjoy it. This is a responsibility we take extremely seriously, and in which we go to great lengths to ensure that high standards are maintained.

In many ways the fact that people can take part in genuine, safe and fairly-paid qualitative research exercises, probably close to where they live and work, remains one of the world's best kept secrets – despite our best efforts to get the word out. There are a lot of sceptics out there who will never believe it, of course, and we're not concerned with trying to convince or persuade them – because who wants a reluctant respondent? Our target is always those who would most definitely be open to it if they only knew.

Outreach work to build our database of participants includes continually developing fresh content and marketing communications, to explain what taking part in research is, and also what it is not. In a world full of hyperbole and deception particularly online standing out effectively is challenging - whilst remaining scrupulously professional and fair: not over-representing potential benefits or earnings for example, when we rigidly restrict repeat attendance, and uphold industry codes of practice with regard to preferred frequencies.

We are the 'public face' of the industry. It is our content that comes up in search results to inform people how to get involved, so that's a heavy weight of responsibility.

We want to make the potential sound attractive and interesting, but also have to be very careful and professional with regard to what we offer or promise.

For every participant you interview in a group, we might be talking to and screening 10 or even 50 times more, depending on how niche your recruit is. Therefore far more people outside the research industry, know about us than they do about the researchers behind it, and they have direct contact with us. That is good as far as future projects are concerned, of course. Incidentally, we are also contacted frequently by people wanting to work professionally in qualitative research and user testing, as a result of our content marketing strategy; we do our best to point them in an appropriate direction.

When we are recruiting a project we may also be representing your client's brand as well.

Saying too much, or the wrong thing, can not only lead to bad and 'leading' recruitment, it can also expose your client's intellectual property to the public – or even to their competitors.

Potentially, it could misrepresent or communicate something negative about their brand, for example by leaking advance disclosure of a product launch or a strategic shift. Even a new ad is generally clearly date-embargoed, and your client doesn't want anybody tweeting about it as a result of seeing a research invitation which shares a little too much about the participants being sought…

We are sometimes quite taken aback by the background information we are given by people working in agencies on behalf of renowned brands, frequently with no NDA or even discussion about confidentiality, and sometimes at the stage when we are just being asked to quote for uncommissioned work. We are always careful to ensure this never makes it to the public domain via our hands, but in an era where every recruiter has access to social media this requires not just careful briefing and control, but high levels of understanding and trust to regulate effectively.

However, even when the end client is successfully 'blinded' and commercial disclosure is not at stake, the way the research industry is represented always takes front and centre position in our external communications. We regard this as our professional role in recruitment, and our responsibility to both the participants and the industry.

We strive at all times to:

- Convey that research events are simply that – no sales, 'sugging', list-building or any other activity will take place, under any circumstances

- Explain the standards and protections in place on participants' behalf, how the Market Research Society Code of Conduct protects them, from research ethics to privacy and confidentiality

- State, with total transparency, expected earnings potential and incentives – including the fact that they cannot take part in paid qualitative, or user, experience more than very occasionally.

- Communicate the direct and indirect benefits of research participation, beyond the money they may earn – like having a genuine chance to influence new brands and services, feed back to providers and shape new products.   As well, hopefully, as sharing interesting conversation and experience.

Choosing a Recruitment Partner

There are many factors to consider when choosing a partner for research participant recruitment. Some of these factors may be completely outside your control, such as timelines and possibly budgets. Other decisions may be needed, perhaps in a hurry, at the outset of a project when decisions have to be made fast, and time for scoping out suppliers is limited.

Obviously I can write in detail only about how things are done at Saros, but the reasons behind those choices are what we hope you find valuable, in choosing with whom you work. There are plenty of projects for which we might not be the best recruiter, and we'd always rather be clear about that and why this is the case

Accountability and Management

Partnership is built on trust, and trust is built on relationship and communication. So there are lots of things to talk about to a potential recruitment supplier about before instructing them

Who is doing the recruiting?

One of the first things to check out when talking to a potential provider, is who will actually be doing the recruitment.

While it might not be unusual for the person delivering the work to be different from the one who quoted on it, we believe that there should be a single senior point of contact at the recruitment firm, project-managing the recruitment, who is personally accountable and up-to-speed with all aspects of the work as it progresses: somebody who keeps updated and understands what is needed and works directly with the interviewers responsible for screening participants personally.

The person selected should be available in an emergency if things change, or need updating. They need to be totally involved in the job as a whole, ready to discuss any aspect of way the job is being managed. It is therefore important to ask questions about the role of outsourcing within the chosen agency because fieldwork companies that work with a minimal internal team still exist.

They are structured to pass things down the line to freelance supervisors working with their own networks of freelance recruitment interviewers. Sometimes they pass work off between one another and, ultimately, it may be impossible to ascertain who is actually working on the project.

Of course plenty of people have worked this way for years, and a couple of decades back this was the only way that work was distributed within the industry, but for the buyer it can have disadvantages to bear in mind. If things go wrong, or are changed, or if updates are needed, it can be difficult getting in touch. Most importantly, in this situation there are more opportunities for communications to fail or for misunderstandings to take place.

You may also have no idea how many people have seen that confidential briefing document or had your email forwarded to them, even if the original contact has signed a confidentiality agreement.

It can be much harder to check whether an agreed screener has been applied and followed correctly, and how work has been quality-controlled and back-checked.

If this structure of delegation and outsourcing is going to be the way in which your work is delivered, you may wish to ask specific questions about how work is progress-chased, how participant history is assessed, how documents are shared and distributed, and how quotas are assessed and co-ordinated. You will need to be clear on who is accountable to you and how updates will be collated and received, and you might also want to ask about how they apply controls against the use of known rogue interviewers.

Although a reputable agency will have their own records of people they will and will not work with, how do they enforce that within the networks they might be using?

Public and professional appearance

Membership of relevant professional bodies is one indicator you might want to examine, for example in the UK is the fieldwork company a Company Partner of the Market Research Society (MRS)?

Are senior staff members Certified members of the MRS and, as such, have they demonstrated competence and knowledge of the industry to the satisfaction of their board?

The MRS, and similar bodies in different markets, also offer award and training schemes, which may be a further indicator plus they offer professional accreditation for industry knowledge.

It's not impossible to manage fieldwork without formal training in the industry of course, but a supplier who has invested in specific qualifications may value professionalism and an opportunity to develop their team.

The Association of Qualitative Research (AQR) is another useful qualitative-specific indicator. While those managing fieldwork are rarely researchers, remaining abreast of industry issues and trends is an important part of fulfilling good service to a knowledgeable client.

Look out for listings in the supplier directory, as well as individual memberships amongst key staff.

If your fieldwork supplier works internationally, or works for international clients within the UK, then you may see other memberships and directory listings as well – the US GreenBook, for example, or ESOMAR.

Even when recruitment happens locally, an awareness of international contexts can be valuable, and you might need suppliers in different markets for different parts of your project.

Publications and conference presentations by senior staff can give you a good indication about the values and standards of an organisation as well, including their extent of investment in professional development and industry presence.

You can also learn more about them, fast, by examining their overall online footprint, including Linkedin profiles and associated recommendations.

All of these, of course, are curated and presented by the individual or their company, and should be read with that in mind, but, when you are choosing a supplier for an important project in a hurry, it's a good place to start, and may be more insightful than what they say on their own online properties.

Of course, you can learn a great deal about many businesses simply from their overall online presence.

In this industry sector, websites can vary a lot in terms of content and communications. You might be want to consider…

- Is their website professionally designed and hosted? Do they look like a credible reliable business?

- If their website is used to recruit members of the public, is the information realistic, professional and responsible? How are they representing the market research industry and the potential of participating in fieldwork to new applicants?

- What do they say about data protection, and does their online presence bear this out? For example, if they are using forms to collect information from either the client or the public, are these SSL secured with a current valid certification?

- Are they appropriately registered as information controllers to the ICO?

- Do they maintain a visible social media presence, which is consistent with all the above? If you monitor their social media, is there an absence of inappropriate disclosure or misleading of participants?

When you buy participant recruitment services, what are you actually buying?

If you're first response is, *"well, that's obvious,"* I'd beg to disagree …based simply on the wide range of expectations – stated and unstated – that clients from different organisations have brought to us over 15 years.

Of course it's our job as the supplier to clarify and qualify those expectations thoroughly as part of the commissioning process, in order to be certain we can deliver exactly what's needed, but the service people require varies a great deal.

For example:

- Do you have a screener written that you want us to deploy word-for-word, or do you want us to develop one based on your persona or list of essential or desirable criteria? Actually, we'd prefer the latter in many ways – but do recognise that, particularly for one branch of a larger or international project, that might not be possible

- Do you have a schedule blocked out for us to which individual sessions are recruited, or do you have a vague list of interviewers' contact details and preferences – which may take a lot longer to co-ordinate, especially if one of them does not like answering emails or is unclear about their movements during the fieldwork period.

- Do you want us to arrange your incentives, your venues, cabs home, restaurants for your clients – yes, we have been asked for that! ...and no, it does not fall within our quoted recruitment cost per head!

- Do you wish to play a role in the recruitment yourselves, for example to review the written long-list of potential applicants before we interview them, or to have a quick call with each of them before they turn up to the main research session? All of this is perfectly possible so long as the timeline permits, and we welcome clients who are sufficiently concerned and involved in the research process to make it happen.

When it comes to a statement of work, we will always need clients to agree with our business terms, which specify roles and responsibilities for a range of scenarios that could affect the recruit – late changes, cancellations, acts of god, data protection, and so on.

Contracting clearly and explicitly for exactly the service you require to be delivered, means that both parties can meet each other's expectations professionally and effectively, with no surprises along the way.

Recruiting participants is a full-time job, and it's one we specialise in exclusively. Other recruiters may have viewing facilities that they prefer to book you into directly, or belong to a network of related companies. Certainly we all know that recruitment is just one element of the service package needed, in order to run your fieldwork smoothly and successfully, and another of other services will need to be sorted out.

For example, incentive handling… Every participant needs to receive an incentive, but we know that some organisations prefer not to handle this directly for a wide range of reasons.

If it makes things run more smoothly, or indeed if there is any doubt at all that participants will receive the amount they are expecting at the time and in the format they were promised, we'd prefer to arrange that directly on the researchers' behalf.

Most people prefer to make their own arrangements for exactly where they want to carry out research, but remember your recruiter is well placed to advise. We have good anecdotal feedback from a wide range of researchers working across the country about different facilities, not to mention comments from many thousands of participants. Although we have no official partnership or recommendation arrangement with any one of them, we are always happy to pass on what we have learned. It's hearsay, because we don't tend to visit these places regularly ourselves but, if you ask us what we think, we'll tell you, and we'll share our feedback from the participants' perspective as well.

Traditional v. Database Recruitment

The biggest change in the participant recruitment industry has been the evolution of first static then online databases, for the storage of participant details. This has led to two different types of provider emerging – but they may not be as different as they initially appear.

The scope of traditional recruitment

The research recruitment industry in the UK was, for decades, based on the tried and tested power of word of mouth.

Indeed it's almost difficult to remember already, but once upon a time, networking was something that happened largely face-to-face, through personal connections. Good recruiters also went out onto the streets with clipboards in the area where the research was to take place, directly intercepting people who seemed likely to fit, and inviting them to screen for upcoming projects.

Back in the 20th century, of course, there was very little data protection legislation to speak of, and if a recruiter met someone they knew might make a terrific participant for something but happened to screen out of the project in hand, well it would make total sense to keep their number, because the right job would come up eventually, one where they'd slot right in. So they typically developed bulging black books and rolodexes. At that time, the word 'database' simply wasn't used very much outside certain kinds of industries, and the people with whom recruiters connected had, generally, some first or second-hand personal relationship.

This was important because a lot of the research itself took place right in their living rooms, as part of the service offered to researchers included the provision of a space to conduct the research, complete with refreshments and hosting. The participants were likely to be drawn from a local area, and it makes sense that the recruiter would prefer to approach people they already knew – or knew by association – if they were intending to invite them into their own home.

While the tools they use have naturally evolved over time, some use similar approaches today, and the best of them combine great interpersonal skills with formidable memories. Many specialise in particular locations, or niches such as medical or executive recruitment, and have built up their extensive contact lists with this in mind.

Traditional recruiters are often criticised for re-using participants too often, for recruiting people known to them, and for 'snowballing' participants by referral from one to another. While we don't tend to work directly with traditional recruiters, we know from our industry experience that there is a huge variation in quality, and that although some bad practice inevitably does go on, many traditional research recruiters work extremely hard at what they do and are very good at it.

When you think about it, it's really hard.

If you went out on the pavement armed with nothing but a clipboard and a pen, to find 2 groups of 8 women who use brand X shampoo, don't reject Y, shop at a certain place and have no allergies to a specific substance, they must fit a particular attitude profile with regard to animal testing view, AND they must be free next Thursday for two hours

– at either 6 or 8:30 but you can't tell them which group they might fit 'til you've run through a 10 minute screener...

Yes, now, if that's OK

...and then I will want to know all about your job and what you earn, even though it doesn't seem all that relevant to washing your hair...

Oh, you have a train to catch?

Well, thanks anyway, yes you have a lovely day too...

How long do you think it'd take you?

How many people would you have to speak to, to fill two groups of 10 for 8 booked, and what would it feel like?

It's not surprising that database recruitment is the convergent methodology, but that can mean many different things - and when buying recruitment services, it is important to understand how potentially ambiguous terms are being used in practice.

Isn't everybody a 'database recruiter' now?

According to dictionary.com the word 'database' is defined as...

"a comprehensive collection of related data organised for convenient access, generally in a computer."

Even as we certainly tend to think in terms of an electronic collection of related data as the definition suggests, I'd argue that the rolodex of a methodical traditional recruiter could have met the definition of the earliest participant recruitment database. She (it was usually a she) would have the contact cards arranged in a searchable sequence, containing different kinds of information in a systematic order –contact information, a bit of demographics, probably some kind of record regarding events they had taken attended. It could be browsed or searched directly, and updated in real time - so long as you had a pen.

So wasn't she a 'database recruiter' all along? Maybe so.

Nowadays, even the most traditional of all these ladies is probably using some kind of electronic version of the above, simply because the tools are available so freely to do so. In that sense, everybody IS a database recruiter – and that makes complete sense, because the job as illustrated above – going out and finding fresh people every time AND taking them through the entire process from a standing start – is not only pretty much impossible in many cases, it's also inefficient. You know when you are talking to a great potential participant, that to let them stroll off into the sunset, simply because they use the wrong brand of shampoo, would be a loss to the industry as a whole.

It also sounds a lot easier in principle to stick up a website and simple data-capture page and encourage people to share their information with you online, rather than pound pavements in the rain. Therefore, these days, pretty much everybody is a database recruiter. What used to be an address book is now at the very least a spreadsheet, often something more complex, and pretty much every freelance recruiter has a website.

This has blurred the lines considerably from what were two quite demarcated approaches a decade or so back, and this is why it's important to ask a lot of questions when choosing a supplier.

For example, you might wish to consider – if they have a database – who is on it? Where did they come from?

Is it a database of past participants, people they have met, a panel they have bought data from?

Or do they invest in recruiting their own resources of fresh people?

Has everybody on their database, specifically, legally opted to be there, for that precise purpose, and is that data stored legally and securely?

If the answers to the final two questions are 'yes', then they might well broadly fit the definition of a database recruiter in a meaningful way. If they simply keep a record of people they've recruited for other jobs, then they have a list of previous participants, and it's really no different from the rolodexes of the 90s. What matters to you is whether they are finding fresh people or not, people who have never taken part in research before, rather than people who have done so - perhaps far too often.

Developing a database

Building a big enough database from which to recruit research events accurately and robustly takes consistent effort, on a continual basis.

When we started doing this at the turn of the millennium, some people argued that a database would not be representative of the population in general and, in particular, would only attract those who were interested enough in technology to use the Internet and Email (these things tended to take capital letters at the time).

It would be of no use in the recruitment of mainstream projects.

We accepted that as valid criticism at the time and actually, in the early days, we recruited thousands of people via paper application forms as well. We had this super-expensive scanner and software that was supposed to save time by recognising handwriting, but didn't always work as well as it should…

We also had a website, of course, because we knew that was going to be important one day.

Nowadays you can safely say that 'users of the internet' do not form a specific distorted demographic of the subset of potential research participants. There are still some segments of society at large who will never now get online, but most strata of the community are fairly well represented in one way or another, and it's the non-users who are unrepresentative.

The difficulty though, is connecting with the right folks online because they are not evenly distributed. 'Build it and they will come' does not work. If you simply put up a website and a Facebook page, you will not build a database at any viable speed and, if you go after the lowest common denominator, chasing people who sign up for every list and competition and panel going, in the interest of numbers – well – that's exactly what you will get.

If you want to attract participants who are not on mailing lists, who are selective about their social media use, people who don't see themselves as looking for 'opportunities' to earn online – if you want a database of real normal people for example, you have to go and find them. You have to do so in a variety of ways, because people are varied.

To some you can pave your way with cold, hard cash, others you get only by actively seeking them out, and asking in the right way.

Our continual investment in developing and recruiting to our database has been one of the cornerstones of our success, and depends upon a number of activities carrying on in parallel.

Social media and content marketing matter a lot of course, and enable us to be present in the conversation where it is taking place; having established profiles on important networks and growing connections, also enhances credibility and enables social proof. Despite all our work for 15 years, there are still plenty of people who don't even know anyone who has taken part in a qualitative research event, who think the whole thing sounds like a bit of a scam or a con.

We have no interest in trying to convince people like this to register with us and give us a go – we don't set out to persuade them that they should. We focus exclusively on the fact that they could, in perfect safety and validity. We want them to come to us when they're ready, not feel pressured or reluctant or 'talked into' anything. Though our arguments are, we hope, attractive and compelling, independent feedback and recommendation is so much more effective. Sharing testimony such as videos of participant feedback, real members of the public who have taken part and enjoyed themselves, really helps to bridge the gap and influence people to get on and sign up.

We use specific ads of course to target required demographics for particular projects, or for ongoing work where we know we have activity coming up – in a new city for example, or with a particular segment we want to boost. These can also be targeted at particular occupations or interest groups, and we also partner with organisations who can represent us authentically and effectively.

Nevertheless, those early detractors were right about one thing to this day – whilst most of the world IS online now, not everybody is willing to sign up and share personal information with brands and organisations they encounter solely in the virtual world. It's not a factor of age particularly, in fact privacy is increasingly important across the spectrum… Sometimes people just feel safer with a brand they can see and touch, or at least meet.

So, we attend community events and talk directly to people about the benefits of research participation. Flyers and leaflets are part of the strategy, as are 'traditional' media ads like print, press and radio. We provide speakers for events, such as those aimed at getting women back into work, helping students in new areas, and flexible working.

We hope that if someone, in an area of interest to us, stumbles across an online ad, then there's a good chance they will have read about us or heard of us in some other way, and will be influenced in their decision to put their hand up and have a go. It makes our ad tracking a lot harder but, actually, we rather like it when people say they can't recall where they first heard about Saros.

If we have become the 'hoover' of market research recruitment in some areas, we are cool with that. Our *what's your opinion worth?* branding has evolved over the years, and as the message gets more generic, that sharing one's insight as a consumer is a transaction of value to both sides, it's all good. Sustaining this however is a continual effort and investment, and is the reason we have a separate team working on this area rather than delivering projects.

We invest a lot in creating content to simply explain how it all works. The profile of qualitative research is so unsung, openly, in comparison to its 'evidence based' sibling, which gets quoted in the mainstream press each day. This works against us all the time, and means that we have to start by explaining what paid qualitative research participation IS and what is it is NOT… Unfortunately, with attendance being rigidly controlled by the 6 month attendance rule, no one is going to 'get rich quick' doing focus groups with us, and while it would be easy to be more noticeable online if we lied and over-promised, we would not compromise the integrity of our brand by doing that.

People learn and take in information in different ways, so we have written material – leaflets, blog posts, press articles and so on. We have videos, of the 'explainer' type, and also of participants sharing their own experiences of taking part.

As well as attending community events 'live', we have friendly people on the phone who can answer queries at the point of registration –because our application form requests quite a lot of personal demographic details, which people unfamiliar with the industry's practices are naturally quite wary about sharing.

These are some of the ways we ensure our database is continually refreshed and, we hope, up to date with the participants we need for the next project. Unfortunately, it doesn't just happen. Although we never know what we will be asked to recruit next, we can of course target our efforts in anticipated directions. For example, if a new client wants to do research in a fresh/relatively untapped area of the UK, we can focus development efforts there for a bit. The more notice we have of upcoming needs, the better job we can do making certain our database is ready to respond effectively.

Recruitment and Screening - not the same thing.

One of the reasons we have a separate team working on the database development to the delivery of each specific project, is that these two disciplines and activities are quite distinct.

Our project managers obviously work closely with the

database team to ensure that the right people are being recruited to enrol with us. Our Research Bookers (a term we chose to distinguish them from the freelance 'Recruiters Network', from whom they are quite different) have nothing to do with finding the right people. They are sent pre-screened interested applicants to telephone interview.

They are NOT under pressure to 'fill it up' and get 'bums on seats' – if we send them 100 potential screened online leads and none of them fit the spec, they can turn around and tell the Project Manager that they have no one to call.

Of course if it's 500 leads and no-one to call, the Project Manager will probably need to talk to the researcher about the reason for that – but our Bookers won't try to bend people to fit, because they have no incentive to do so.

Similarly, if there appear to be plenty worth calling but they don't check out on the phone, then they don't get booked in. Because our Bookers don't waste time calling people who are ineligible on the factual stuff (age, location, brands etc.), they can really concentrate on rigorously checking the 'softer' factors – motivation, commitment, awareness – the less tangible things, that can make all the difference between a good-enough group and a 'wow' group.

They don't have to spend time explaining what research is, why people should take part, why they won't get sold anything or spammed, or what time it starts; or trying to persuade someone who has just sat down to dinner or TV that they really want to be doing this next Thursday instead.

This is fundamental to the way Saros was designed from the start, because we identified that these two activities – recruitment and screening – were very different. Mixing them up was inefficient, potentially detrimental to good recruitment, and created conflicting priorities. We prefer to keep things simple and clear, in the best interests of both researchers and participants.

For us, this is one of the key differentiators between traditional and database recruitment.

When the same individual is under pressure to both find and screen people for a job (usually with a very tight specification and deadline), then something is more likely to give. Either they resort to previously found people they know might fit the spec, (which could result in re-using people too often) – or they are too easily driven to flex the fit to the spec slightly, just a little bit ...to avoid going through the screener properly, in case it takes too many people out. Under this sort of pressure, perhaps there simply isn't time to explain to completely fresh people everything they need to know about taking part, or worse it might be tempting to give just out a tiny bit too much info including what the 'right' answers are...

Another difficulty with the single freelancer traditional model too, is the lack of supervision that allows this to happen. Whilst there are defined industry procedures for back-checking a proportion of interviews according to the quantitative interviewing method, there is no oversight of the actual recruitment process itself – how the screener is used, how many people screen out, or what is being asked or explained about the research. We find a more transparent structure, with at least two people seeing every screener response and profile completed, makes more clear and effective screening. It also allows for much quicker troubleshooting if there are any problems or discrepancies at any point during the recruitment or afterwards.

Is a participant database the same as a panel?

From time to time we get asked about our 'panel' of research participants. This is a label we are keen to avoid however, because it can lead to confusion and misunderstanding.

A qualitative recruitment database is not a "research panel" in any sense, or it certainly should not be.

Research panels are generally used in quantitative research, to provide responses to surveys online. As such, they are managed completely differently from our database. Sometimes panels are rented out to third parties, and participants on it might be sent large numbers of surveys to complete. Usually, data about the composition of the panel is made public to potential purchasers/hirers.

Panels are recruited and managed in all sorts of ways, and there are undoubtedly many different standards within them. The ability to recruit and manage panels online has meant that, for quantitative work, the question and response lifecycle time has been drastically reduced – surveys can be sent and questions answered extremely fast, perhaps within hours. There are known issues around motivation for joining, and how many different panels people can join – indeed, there are websites and companies specialising in selling lists of good survey panels to join ('good' generally referring to earning potential), and going as far as to instruct people about lucrative survey opportunities and the qualifying responses needed to participate.

This makes it very difficult for legitimate and ethical panel providers, because they have no control over the portals via which people are referred to join them. We have occasionally found Saros being added to one of these sites based on total misunderstanding of what it is we do, and we always fight to get such links removed. Nobody should have to pay to be able to take part in market research under any circumstances, but when the hosted services are outside the UK it's difficult to get action taken. Sometimes we get a flood of students from the other side of the world attempting to register with us in the hope of paid surveys (which we do not have).

For qualitative recruitment, it's not about the numbers, or the turnaround. We will never publish demographic information about the content of our database, because it would not be meaningful for anyone to know anyway. If we said we had X number of people in a certain postal sector in the C2D category, that would tell you nothing about whether we could recruit your project there, basing it on a particular profile of product use and attitudes. Instead we use knowledge of our database composition internally to decide whether a recruit is viable for us to take on - given what we know about the product penetration, how far people are likely to travel to take part in that area, how long we have to network outside of our database if necessary, and so on.

Qualitative not Quantitative.

Because the people joining us are applying for face to face events, we double-check the information they shared in their registration very carefully, at the point of recruitment for any specific project.

People's demographic data can update at any time, when they get a new job or change their domestic circumstances. We know that what matters to our clients is the precise status of their participant the day they take part in research, not what they said when they signed up for some panel a few years ago.

Of course we can and, from time to time, do recruit quantitative projects from our database – more often than not for existing clients, and frequently as part of a combined project with qual and quant elements - but we are careful to ensure that our database is not overused, that it doesn't become a panel of regular survey participants. Although the techniques and approaches used in qual and quant are very different, we do believe that being a part of a frequently-used survey panel must inevitably change somebody's natural responses to questionnaires, which could impact the way they complete our screeners. We don't want people attracted to register with us for the purpose of earning payments and prizes for filling things in, who are driven by that sole motivation for enrolling; we don't actually find that's a great fit with being an effective and engaged qualitative participant, and we're keen to keep our position quite separate and distinct.

We have heard of panel company data being used to recruit for qualitative and user experience projects with some success, and perhaps for some projects it might be a viable approach. So much would depend on the quality, validity and segmentation of the panel itself, as well as the incidence of the desired recruit. It also depends on the resources available to screen the participants effectively on the phone, and double-check all the relevant responses given, ensuring effective fit and commitment from each participant before they are booked in. So a participant database is not a panel, they don't contain the same people and they are not used for the same purposes.

When traditional recruitment works best

We are database recruiters, and have detailed above what we regard to be the advantages of that method over the old traditional networked approach. However, it's fair to say that there ARE occasions when we have to hold up our hands and say, we are not the best supplier to recruit this – what you need are 'boots on the ground', armed with clipboards and a smile.

One example of this would be recruiting via directly observed behaviour.

If a researcher needs to interview customers who pick up and look at a product in-store but ultimately do not purchase it, it would be very difficult to recruit this reliably asking about their recalled actions, of which they may not have adequate awareness. In this case it would make more sense to sit and observe exactly what the shoppers are doing at the fixture itself, before intercepting those exhibiting the behaviour of interest right at that moment. Now, in this scenario the researcher might not need the presence of a recruiter at all, and be fine to observe and intercept their own participants as they go along, but if the required behaviour is very rare or complex, or involves watching two areas of a store at the same time, then a traditional recruitment firm with a field force would be best placed to provide an interviewer.

Similarly, if the location is paramount – for example if you need to recruit users of a specific rural post office.

We could easily recruit you users of rural post offices in a particular county using our database-driven approach, but if only one location interests you then that's not likely to work, because we simply won't have that entire village's cohort of pensioners on our database. It would be far more effective to have an interviewer or two standing right outside the door, ready to talk to people as they step outside clutching their stamps.

If this is not possible there may be a way we can work with the branch itself to facilitate recruitment - for example we have had sales staff at a retail outlet include a leaflet in each carrier bag, inviting shoppers to apply for focus groups to help improve their forthcoming ranges.

This worked pretty well in terms of finding regular and recent shoppers, and followed our preferred inbound/opted-in approach. Rather than research recruitment butting into their shopping trip with a clipboard, they could read about it and contact us in a way, and at a time, to suit themselves. It also meant we got actual shoppers, which was what was required, rather than browsers and tyre kickers.

But unless you can involve local personnel in this way, then the clipboard intervention would be the best way to intercept people you know have shopped in that branch on that day.

A final case where a traditional recruitment company

would be a better approach than using us, is where an extensive telephone list must be cold-called.

Although we have developed some very effective ways of working with customer lists, the one thing we don't have is a call centre. If you have a large list, no email addresses on it, and a short timescale in which to recruit from it, then you need more than one interviewer working the same list. You therefore need a call centre with call-management software, logging the outcome of each contact and updating it centrally, and central updates of recruitment accomplished across the different quota cells.

This kind of set-up is generally more applicable to quantitative interviewing than to qual, but there are times when, for example, a number of in-depth interviews must be scheduled from a client list, and on these occasions we would always recommend the use of a firm with the right set-up to achieve this.

Specialist Recruiters, Specialist Participants?

Whichever approach taken – database, personal networking, or a blend of the two – there are recruitment services that specialise in recruiting particular kinds of participant, often within very tight niches. These specialists most definitely have a role, particularly when recruitment is needed within a precisely defined professional specialism, and where specific knowledge and expertise is useful for distinguishing between these experts and screening them effectively for research.

For example, within the medical sphere, there are many firms who focus on building networks of consultants and senior registrars at specific institutions, and also primary care professionals. They are able to target not only the professionals themselves, but because of regular contact and networking they are able to reach out through them to recruit patients with rare conditions and treatment plans.

The relationship of trust they have established with the medics means they are able to connect quickly and find even very low incidence illnesses, and that the referral made will be a medically correct and authoritative one. Often such recruiters will have some medical background of their own, which enables them to create effective screeners which will deliver good recruitment underpinned by specialist understanding.

Saros generally takes the position that whilst recruiters might be specialised, participants are not. An applicant may be a cardio-thoracic consultant who would be ideal for a project coming up once every 5 years looking at applied surgical techniques, but she may also be a user of a salon haircare brand who are recruiting for ad testing, as well as a mid-late adopter of a family games console who are re-launching a media tie-in title for Christmas. So far as we are concerned, she is a potential applicant for any of these projects - and indeed she might well prefer talking in research about games or shampoo, as opposed to the day job. At the end of the day, potential participants are rounded individuals, with varied and complex behaviours and attitudes – and we don't believe in siloing them within our database as only being appropriate for a particular kind of project. What people feed back to us is how much they appreciate the variety of opportunities being part of Saros offers them. One time they get to test a mobile app, then next year they are part of an online community project about baby feeding, a further project might invite them to an in-depth interview about how they select software at work.

Of course we have to explain to them why their opinions as an IT specifier may be deemed to be worth twice as much to the researcher as they are when speaking as a grocery shopper, but we are always completely transparent about that, and if they won't get out of bed for potential consumer projects after taking part in a much rarer B2B one, then that is entirely their call.

So recruitment can be very specialised, but participants not so much. They may have as much to say about current affairs, how they shop, holidays and their family as they do about their work in the consulting room or board room and we prefer to offer them that choice.

We do, however, see a role for specialism in the way projects are managed. One reason our team loves working agency-side is the variety of work that we get to deal with, far more than any one participant will get to see. Very often a new recruitment brief will have us quickly scrambling through Google, or picking colleagues brains urgently, even before we can cost it up – because there is a sense in which every new project we do requires us, rapidly, to become a bit of an expert in that subject, to align ourselves with the end client's product and sphere of influence briefly, in order to be able to develop an effective route to screening.

Within the team we have clear areas of expertise, passion even, when it comes to certain areas of technology. It would be difficult to manage complex games testing recruits without a very solid grounding in the state of the market (and personal motivation to remain abreast of new developments), the same goes for mobile technology. It is always useful to be able to empathise with the lives of certain participants, such as parents of young children or experienced travellers.

Others might have professional experience in a range of useful areas: Saros always recruits teams based on their aptitude and attitude for work done rather than for experience within the research industry itself – on the basis that the latter can always be taught whilst the former cannot (Saros also prefers to train someone in the way we work from scratch, rather than having to change habits acquired elsewhere). This has led to the development of a team with a wide range of career histories, from finance and travel to education and community sector work. This is invaluable when it comes to understanding specialist proposals - and ensures that the right questions are asked, at every stage, from costing the recruit through to confirming the participants.

So, work is occasionally subcontracted to specialised recruiters – for example, to recruit endocrinologists working for a specific health authority or something, a whole job will be referred on to them. Internally, we treat each project as a unique opportunity to match to the best participants and managed by the person with best fit for overall experience and understanding to get it off to a flying start.

Briefing Your Recruiter

In order to do our best work – and find the right participants to help YOU do your best work - it is essential that a thorough briefing takes place at the outset.

Schedule and Logistics

Recruiting for qualitative research or user experience can in many ways be regarded as event management.

There are various dates and deadlines, activities that have to come together successfully by that point, resources to be managed, and a critical path through it all which needs to be maintained. Successful project management requires a lot of things to happen, some of which occur in sequence, others can be paralleled…

Getting the briefing right underpins everything else and ensures that the project is set up correctly from the outset.

When do we have to decide…?

When we take on a project to recruit and state a minimum timeline, the clock can only start running when we have the essentials necessary to get the screener designed and potential participants invited.

That means pretty much everything has to be nailed down in terms of precisely who we are going to recruit.

We have to have our target defined, otherwise it is not possible to write a screener to identify them or be sure that we can find them.

In terms of location, we need to know the general area at the outset, because this also affects who we will target to invite, and it also means that applicants can make an informed choice as to whether they will want to travel to the venue or not.

We always advise making incentives available at a flat rate, without additional transport costs – other than in exceptional circumstances (involving disabled participants, for example), so it's only fair to be able to tell people pretty clearly where the research is going to take place.

However, if the exact venue is still being pinned down, for now it might be OK to launch without the address. We will need it as soon as we start booking people in as confirmed participants, but if it takes an extra day or so then that's fine.

So long as we can be fair and realistic in advising participants though, which means being as specific as we can. *"Central Brighton"* is pretty clearly defined, but *"Central London"* is not quite enough...

Someone who works in the West End might well consider it's not worth the hassle after all, when the venue turns out to be in the city. The exact address is never disclosed to anybody, until they are definitely confirmed and booked into the group, and validation performed.

When it comes to time slots, again it's helpful if the

project can be launched with the schedule known and agreed. People have complicated lives and commitments and, when the time comes, simply knowing whether they are free or not on Wednesday evening might not be enough – not if they have to get home to take over from a child-carer, or don't finish work 'til a fixed time. It's frustrating for all concerned if they apply for something and then ultimately cannot make it due to a practical limitation, like an inconvenient start time.

However, if we are booking in a series of depth interviews for example, or user tests over a period, then we can launch without the precise timings nailed down, if we have to. Being able to say, *"there are a series of hour-long interview slots taking place throughout the working day only, on Tuesday 28th through to Thursday 30th"*, should be enough to give people an idea of whether to bother applying or not.

Researchers' and Respondents' schedules

When it comes to schedules, we appreciate that there are a number of potentially conflicting pressures here.

In particular, you might have access to certain facilities or resources at particular times, and you might have diary and travel issues of your own that make evening working impractical.

Your clients who want to observe the research have their own preferences and schedules to keep.

However, if you want to attract a representative sample of working people, for a project of any size, we would argue that you simply have to make some sessions available to take place outside of the working day.

Of course not everyone works a typical 9-5 office day.

There are flex-timers, part-timers, mature students, shift workers and everything in between. These all represent some kind of slight difference to the majority, the average working person (and average consumer of your client's brand or target market) but not in any negative way. Saros has been actively promoting flexible and remote working for many years. However, we do know that on those occasions when having to go into London for a meeting, the majority of the world still moves according to fairly predictable rush (or shuffle-along) hours, and work tends to fit around this.

So, if you want to do your sessions during the day, they are going to be recruited from people who either don't work this kind of schedule, or who are sufficiently senior or flexible enough to take time out of their working day to attend. They won't be drawn from the full potential pool of applicants that would otherwise be available, and wouldn't necessarily be completely representative of that pool of people.

This doesn't mean it can't be recruited, and often is. If we believe that it's open enough to be viable we will make sure it gets done, but they won't be 'typical' participants. They might be very good respondents – people from creative industries, for example, often work flexibly and can bring great insights and ideas to the right kind of research. Then again, if your target market is predominantly made up of people whose lives are quite ordered and structured, what you could end up with is a group that is a perfect match for the recruitment spec, but simply doesn't look and feel totally right or typical.

The other possibility of course is that if the requirements are very niche and challenging to start with, the need to do it during the working day might tip it from challenging to impossible. We may not know this until we get it out there and see, but it's a risk on a very tight recruit.

Whilst some people have great discretion over their working hours and can easily put a meeting in the diary if keen to attend a research project, others will suddenly have a 'dentist appointment' or whatever, if they do not have this kind of flexibility.

That is between them, their employer and their conscience of course, but we want to ensure that the contributions you are hearing in your research event are based on face-value truthfulness as far as humanly possible. Starting the whole thing off with the need for any deception seems to us to go against the spirit of openness and honesty we want to encourage in the session.

Although working hard to make your research event as enticing and attractive as possible to potential participants, we definitely don't encourage anyone to tell lies – before, during or after the session. So please, if you possibly can, try to have some sessions in the evening, out of typical work time. If you can do both, then so much the better – particularly if you want to attract non-working parents, daytime sessions are great but please make them mornings or lunchtimes, if the intention is to attract home-makers with school aged children.

We often receive draft schedules with sessions at 4, 6 and 8pm for example, based purely around a convenient block-booking at a viewing facility, but 4pm is actually a dreadful time to recruit for, because most working people can't easily leave work that easily, and anyone who looks after school-age children is definitely out.

Far better to make it a 12 noon session. You might get a few working people making their lunchtime stretch a bit, and you'll be able to involve those with parenting and domestic commitments as well. Put on some sandwiches, and everyone will be happy.

What about weekends? Well, these can work particularly well for research with families and young people. Indeed, with younger children as participants, it's difficult to do a lot without weekend slots. Young people's lives seem so full these days with hours of homework to fit in around various extra-curricular activities, and often there are siblings and other children to consider, as well as external care-providers.

Getting a youngster brought to a research facility on a school day might be almost impossible, and certainly getting a group of them there at one time, or more than one individual session conducted per night, might be a logistical challenge impossible to overcome.

So weekends can be good, but we need to be careful with assumptions about public transport.

Sundays in particular can be the worst day for finding engineering works and disruptions, often scheduled at irritatingly short notice – just as everyone is booked and confirmed you suddenly learn that the station serving the venue is closed all day, with a replacement bus service which drives a double-decker right through your careful scheduling.

A few discreet calls early in the project set-up might well head this kind of chaos off at the pass.

All in all, scheduling requires a bit of thinking from the participants' point of view, and a healthy dose of realism and common-sense. Bear in mind that the respondents' profession might make certain times of year very different from others – the run-up to the end of the financial year in the Spring is a difficult time to get hold of finance professionals, especially IFAs who are busy trying to make the most of their clients' allowances for this and that.

Journalists and policy people are driven, in their sphere, by public events such as the parliamentary calendar, the most intriguing research event in the world will not compete with state events. Teachers simply *cannot* attend research during the daytime during term time, and find evenings difficult as well. Catch them during the school holidays instead, for a much better reception. Medical professionals are exceptionally busy at all times, however they do work curious shifts, so can be available at odd times during the day…

If you really need people in the daytime and it is not business-specific research, why not look at recruiting on behaviour alone, and letting the occupational status fall out as it may? We have received briefs before that say 'no housewives, no students' for groups during the day, because high-status brands are involved and the client is perhaps convinced that only working women might be their customers. That is to disregard immediately, and eliminate, whole swathes of people, from those early retired to independently wealthy, who might have contributed valuable insights to a group on luxury brands, *and* be free to attend it.

A student these days can be anybody – certainly not necessarily a hand-to-mouth 18-year-old undergraduate. All too often it seems that buyers/specifiers of research are thinking of their own student experiences, which may – dare we say it – be from some time ago. The students we typically recruit nowadays as research participants are often very hard-working portfolio people, who not only greatly appreciate the incentive of a chance to earn, but have plenty to contribute from experience of life and business.

Any recruitment agency will be glad to discuss the impact of scheduling on the likely outcome of recruitment, and offer practical advice and suggestions about how and when to engage the best participants to meet the client's desired outcomes. The viability of a given recruit might well depend, in the final event, on when you can actually see participants.

Timelines and critical paths

One way to view the participant recruitment process is as a project management task. A project is made up of activities and resources and schedules. Certain things on the schedule can happen simultaneously, others have to follow on, one from another. There are a limited number of critical paths through the range of options, and if you change one element it can have a knock-on effect on everything, including the potential delivery date. It could be that something else is flexible and squashy enough to absorb a bit of alteration, even if one thing IS changed... It depends.

For example, the administration of venue booking can take place alongside the setting up of a screener and the screener cannot be signed off as complete until the dates for each town have been finalised – that's a milestone on the critical path. You cannot attempt to move beyond it until that is ticked off. If you make changes later, it means re-cycling back to that point, with resources having been wasted.

At other times you might have to look for flexibility in the project plan overall. If the screener sign-off is delayed by 3 days, it might not be possible to contract the recruitment time sufficiently to get the job done but, if there is a 7-day pre-task in the timeline, then it might be possible to stay on track by simply accepting that some participants will be doing a 5-day pre-task instead, if they are recruited later in the process.

Perhaps the pre-task could, in fact, be accomplished over a much shorter time period, by allowing for reflective completion rather than in-the-moment? It might not be ideal from a research point of view, but if you would be open to flexibility on this with a last-minute replacement, then it's better to consider all options at the outset.

Above all, good project management has some contingencies built into it somewhere. If the lead time gets squeezed before the job even starts ...then there's a problem with the venue ...then someone decides there's got to be a change on the screener – and so on – there is nowhere to go with it; something has to give. If there's nothing else with any slack in it, then that's going to end up being the end date, because there isn't anywhere else to go.

Of course, hopefully, on a lot of recruitment jobs, the timeline is pretty simple.

Here's the brief... We want these people to turn up at this venue in a fortnight's time.

Not a lot can go wrong or get off the rails there, assuming they exist then give us the spec and we will go and recruit them.

We would never expect to have to revisit that delivery date in any shape or form, unless the design is complex. If they have to spend a certain amount of time on an online task before meeting face to face, or the client is determined to view the groups taking place at the most awkward time

– then please consider building in a day or so of slack up-front in the timeline, just in case.

Apart from anything else, things can change or go wrong; product samples aren't available to be shipped; the courier loses a quarter of them; the online platform crashes; a hurricane is forecast, or a wildcat tube strike throws a spanner in the whole works!

Putting a day or two's contingency into the timelines can make all the difference, to what is or is not possible in these circumstances, so it's well worth considering up-front.

Where will your fieldwork take place?

Although you may not have to decide this at the point of commissioning, sooner or later we'll need to agree exactly where your research event is going to take place.

You might have access to appropriate facilities at your location, such as a viewing room or user testing lab, in which case it's easy. Or we can, of course, recruit into any venue anywhere in the UK, if you need to take your fieldwork out and about. However, we would always argue strongly in favour of using professional viewing facilities, and failing that a neutral public location.

There is a strong tradition in the UK of using domestic locations for research, in particular the living rooms of traditional recruiters, who in addition to recruiting participants act as hosts on the night for the actual sessions. However, this is rarely appropriate when participants are recruited truly independently of each other, via database-driven recruitment. We have surveyed our members on this point, because we did in the past used to recruit into domestic locations, but the overwhelming feedback we received was that going to a stranger's home is really rather uncomfortable and weird, particularly for participants who are new to research. This makes perfect sense when you think about it

We have seen it argued that viewing facilities are very unnatural and sterile places to conduct research, compared to a domestic location. Well there may be some truth in this, but that very neutrality actually levels the playing field far more effectively than the random qualitative variables introduced by the presence of a stranger's domestic stuff. Some viewing facilities are more 'homely' than others – from a design point of view; some are, intentionally, very comfortably domestic, whereas others are more office-like and professionally orientated. We're always happy to advise where we can, about appropriate locations in different areas.

It's also been suggested that for certain categories of participant, a viewing facility might be overwhelming or intimidating, and this could be true in very limited categories –such as children, or vulnerable adults. Having seen this argument applied to research with retired people or housewives however, that is simply patronising in the extreme, and we'd always counter this with the feedback we have received from participants with various backgrounds.

We do appreciate that viewing facilities aren't cheap, and not every bit of fieldwork needs to be viewed either directly or remotely. In that case, it's easy to hire a room in a community centre, bar or hotel – depending on the kind of group and what is appropriate for the participants.

These can range from very cheap-as-chips to not much less than you would end up paying for a viewing facility, once you factor in things like hotel prices for refreshments, and the need to have a host present on the night – hotel reception staff seem to be notoriously bad at directing clients and participants reliably to the correct room, always changing shift at the most awkward moment, and an extra pair of hands is essential. (Making sure that the second group people doesn't burst in on the first is another reason to have a colleague with you on the night, even if no clients are present.)

Don't overlook the potential of public buildings, every town hall has the list of rooms available to hire throughout their area, ranging from formal meeting-spaces to backrooms in libraries and stately homes, with some very cost-effective options to consider.

Is it ever appropriate to do research in someone's home? Well of course it is, if it's their *own* home, or they are the lead participant in a friendship pair or something. When it comes to children, it saves your having to pay a chaperone fee to a parent or guardian, because they are there already (although depending on the child and the subject, they could be more easily distracted in their own place)

It might even be useful in context to the research itself, being able to see their consumer electronics set up in the den, or poking around and taking videos in kitchen cupboards. We are always amazed what respondents will agree to let researchers do in the name of research... We have even had an ethnographer sitting on a participant's toilet lid, interviewing and taking photos whilst she shaved her legs – you couldn't really do that in a viewing facility.

If it's a depth interview, particularly one not needing to be directly observed, it's highly likely that participants will feel most at home and settled in their own space, and be pleased to make the researcher welcome. It gives them a sense of control and also privacy, which can aid disclosure for research that might be quite probing and sensitive.

One thing to bear in mind however, particularly if you are considering inviting other people into a participant's home or taking clients with you, is public liability insurance. Hotel rooms and viewing facilities always have cover, as well as certified standards and qualified personnel for the provision of refreshments and AV equipment. In our experience, many individuals offering their living rooms as focus group hosts cannot offer this.

If you have insurance of your own to protect you if someone falls down a host's stairs, feels ill after eating a sandwich or electrocutes themselves on their DVD player, then hopefully it won't be a worry, but it's alarming how many people cheerfully seem to overlook this requirement, on the basis that nothing has ever gone wrong before.

Of course, as recruiters, the location is not our call - and once basic health and safety is established we will always do our best to recruit for you exactly where you want to do it. The only thing we need from you is the address and directions, so that we can do everything within our power to get the participants to your door right on time, as well as a phone contact your end for use on the day.

Naturally, we have details of most of the main viewing facilities stored in our database and a set of directions, which we know work, and are clear and understandable to participants. If the research is taking place somewhere new to us such as your offices, then it really does make a difference to get total clarity on directions – down to the level of, *"Come out of exit 7 at the tube station, then walk down High St 'til you see an estate agent with a yellow shop-front, where there is the left-turn into Research*

Road".

A journey you do every day will be completely unfamiliar to a perhaps slightly nervous participant, and we want to ensure their route is bulletproof.

Of course, we'll go grab some Street View images and maps and do our best, but you will know the little details that we don't.

A phone number is essential too, and we encourage participants to print and bring their confirmation email with them when they come to their research. A great many of them do get confused, perhaps if they have applied for lots of research events with us and finally get selected to participate, they are convinced that they are coming to do research 'at Saros'.

We do make it very clear that this is not the case and they need to ask for your named individual contact on the day, along with the company or description of the research...but, chances are, even if they have this printout in their hand when they get off the bus, that it's our interviewer's phone number, (the last in their phone from the reminder call they received an hour ago) – to say, "*I can't find you*".

The better the quality of the information you share with us, the greater is our chance of being able to direct them to your front door, if they face difficulties.

The vast majority do not have any problem, but we'd rather be secure in the expectation of a 100% turnout; some – not excluding creative, imaginative and excellent research respondents are – for some reason – hopeless with written directions.

Telling Participants about the Research

"This Saros Research Project is all about…"

One vital thing to clarify before recruiting starts, is the official purpose of the research and how we should refer to it. Hopefully we will have a clear idea what the research is *actually* about from your briefing, but that is not the same as the public label we will use to invite applicants for it. We'll need to find and agree something slightly different.

Usually this is a simple case of using good, blind-recruitment practice, and naming the research after a broad category rather than the brand. 'Chocolate research', 'haircare research', 'mobile apps research' etc. are all simple shorthand for the topic as a whole, completely fair and not misleading to participants. They can work out that the research is probably on behalf of one of the brands or manufacturers in, for instance, the chocolate industry and not a curious academic, keen to take the pulse of the typical shopper's attitude towards cocoa-based confectionary.

We know that during the research event itself, it will probably become pretty obvious who the research sponsor is, and that the group is taking a slightly narrower focus than previously suggested – the moment of 'reveal' might even be a fundamental part of the discussion guide, so we'd never compromise that by leaking it during recruitment. Instead we'll agree a mutually acceptable category-based label to use. If we happen to have a run of projects on similar topics, we'll need to agree some artistic licence to mix things up a little, otherwise people won't be motivated to apply, thinking it's a previous project they applied for unsuccessfully.

The need to blind might be more about behaviour than brand however, particularly if that behaviour is less aspirational or socially desirable. For example, if you want to talk to people who are regular users of your online sales platform whose feedback rating has dropped by a factor of one point over the past 12 months, but who have the attitude of being an exemplar user with intention to continue trading.

That all makes sense, but we aren't going to put a shout out for 'lazy sellers research'.

Between us we will need to agree how much the participants can be told about the research; on what it is going to centre and how to attract those who are going to be the best fit. Words really matter... Women may be encouraged to apply for anti-ageing skincare research, but we've been sent screeners that suggest we tell people we'd like talk to them about 'wrinkle cream'!

The whole area of healthy behaviour and diet is also very difficult. If we need to recruit people who feed their children total rubbish, careful choice of language is essential so that they feel free to be completely honest in their responses even if, deep down, they know it's not what they should be doing and they'd rather be kidding us as well as themselves.

Sometimes, of course, there are marketing factors involved on our part, when it comes to trying to attract people to apply for your research event. Some topics have rather more glamour to them than others, and one of the most (or do I mean least?) memorable projects we had to recruit for was on behalf of a brand of wallpaper adhesive. Not exactly sexy, on the page, and we talked about how to make participating in it sound slightly more exciting, without being misleading or disingenuous to potential participants.

On reflection, the discussion guide did centre a lot around why people chose certain products to use in creating the home they loved and, between ourselves and the client we agreed that 'home interior decorating research' would have a greater chance of attracting the right people. Careful screening followed, naturally, to ensure they had actually used separate wallpaper adhesive on a domestic project in the past year and could talk about the products and brands and why they'd chosen them …but had we suggested they might want to come and discuss glue for 2 hours, we might, I fear, have had a fairly low uptake.

We monitor and split-test click-through rates to the application form sometimes, using different descriptions and subject lines.

Given that we have to send invitations out by email, we occasionally have to resort to linguistic gymnastics to avoid tripping spam filters, such as when we had a recruit that was tricky enough in the first place, about medication for erectile dysfunction. Just about every word we could use to describe what we needed in terms of symptoms and medications was a red flag in our mail broadcast system, and we wondered if we'd have to resort to the kind of contrived misspellings that fill our spam traps daily! It took a while to work out a form of neutral words that met the aspired-to transparency principles but had some chance of reaching the main inbox of potential participants.

Financial research is another one that needs better PR as genre, because so many people regard the entire area as a necessary evil rather than something they are actively interested in.

It can be difficult not to fall back on the marketing of

the industry itself – no-one is going to fall for 'freedom planning research' or some-such flannel. In general, we make an effort to be honest, and find some benefit or interest in it for them – hopefully not just the incentive on offer, but sometimes that really does sound like the best thing about it.

Consumer technology recruitment can bring different challenges, in terms of how we describe research projects to participants.

We are frequently looking to recruit users of various products, services and technologies they use without much thought or expertise, because they are consumer goods designed to be used in this way, every day. User testers in particular cannot confine their research to enthusiastic geeks, they need to know that people at all levels of technical ability are going to be able to click on their app and make it work as soon as it downloads, or take their fitness tracker out of the box and be up and running fast, without needing lengthy manuals or support calls.

If, however, you say you want to invite them to communications app testing, a lot of late adopters or even mainstream users might be put off applying, thinking, *"But I don't know anything about that!"* Instead, it's often more effective to choose a fairly bland and benign title like 'keeping in touch on your smartphone', and then drill down into the apps they use and how frequently, during screening itself.

At least with technology people are usually fairly happy to declare a lack of aptitude and understanding, in contrast to financial and investment matters for example, where there seems to be greater fear of revealing ignorance – so the way people are invited to research needs to be handled very differently across these two verticals.

There might be political or other reasons for deliberately obscuring the subject of the research, and we sometimes have to remind clients that the label we are seeking to identify here will be seen by all long-listed potential applicants for the project – this is a far, far greater number than those actually screened in, and involved. It could be thousands more, and any of those people can also forward the call to action on, to whoever they want.

So if there is likely to be any commercial sensitivity, social controversy or whatever, we'd rather keep things as neutral as possible at the very top of the recruitment funnel as this represents. One example was in recruitment of people likely to be affected by a proposed high-speed rail link, which had attracted a lot of media attention… In this case we recruited scrupulously on travel behaviour for our 'business travel research', leaving it entirely to the researchers and their clients to present their identity to the participants themselves after they had been welcomed to the project and NDAs signed.

Occasionally however, we have to decline a potentially deceptive brief, which could harm participants. We won't lie in recruitment, at least not by commission. There have also been occasions where greater disclosure from the client to ourselves would have enabled us to discuss a better choice of presentation.

An example of this was a research project we were asked to recruit about retirement planning, which turned out, in the end, to be almost entirely centred around the subject of legacies, wills and inheritances. We could see no reason to have obscured this point in recruitment anyway …and this led to our having to deal with a very upset participant the following day, a man whose wife had died a few months prior to the research event. As it turned out, it was one of his first attempts to do something sociable outside the home since that time.

Had we been aware of the content of the discussion guide, he could have been sensitively screened out during recruitment as completely unsuitable for the project in question, or given a chance to consider whether this was an area he was totally comfortable speaking about in a group, well in advance, with plenty of time to withdraw if he changed his mind on that matter. As it was he found himself trapped in a roomful of strangers surrounded by all this highly triggering discussion, and a researcher who found his 'emotional comments' to be 'very unhelpful to the group dynamic'!

Whenever there is any potential sensitivity involved, which might affect some participants significantly more than others, - causing them to be adversely affected by their research participation in violation of the Market Research Society Code of Conduct - we will always insist on complete transparency with participants. 'Alcoholic drinks research', not 'food and drink' or 'lifestyles research' - because if we end up recruiting religious abstainers, recovering alcoholics or a date-rape victim, it might well be disruptive in your research event, as well as a disturbing experience for the individual concerned. This has occasionally led to delicate negotiations with clients concerned about issues of priming as well as brand-blinding, but there are some categories of research where the potential for individual harm is higher than in others and requires careful handling.

So, the simple matter of what to say about the aim of a research project, might require more thought than anticipated. It falls firmly into the category of things that need to be decided before a project can be launched.

Confidentiality and Non-Disclosure Agreements

We talk a lot about how we endeavour to protect your confidentiality when it comes to publishing information and invitations to research events, but we are well aware that far greater detail is revealed to participants when they actually take part in research. Instead of one email or tweet they are going to be exposed to hours of direct stimulus and conversation about your new products and ideas... Much of which will be valuable and sensitive commercial material.

We are often surprised how perfunctorily this is sometimes addressed, by clients and researchers, and it is something upon which we conducted internal research ourselves in 2014. We surveyed 400 recent participants across a range of different events we had recruited, and followed up by conducting detailed interviews with those who had interesting stories.

Our findings indicated that although participants generally felt that their own confidentiality was well-respected and protected in their research participation, there was more confusion about what was expected of them in return. They were generally aware that some things weren't to be talked about outside of the session, but they often weren't sure what, nor could they clearly recall how or when they had been instructed /advised about this.

Generally, we find participants feel quite privileged at the extent of what is revealed to them in research, particularly if it means an opportunity to peek behind the curtain or glimpse the future plans of a brand they know and love. And sometimes they get very excited about that, and want to talk about it afterwards... Human nature. So we would argue that it's very important that what is and isn't OK to talk about is made very clear to participants throughout the process, and reinforced both by us in recruitment and yourselves at the introduction to the session.

One way to stress the importance of avoiding inappropriate sharing is to use a non-disclosure agreement (NDA), and your organisation may well already have one on file for standard use (if not, there are many model documents available). But the difficulty here is that these tend to be written by lawyers, rather than researchers or normal human beings; they can be rather daunting in length and verbosity.

Remember that the intention of getting this document signed in this instance is to avoid inappropriate leaks, *not* to give legal recourse after damage has been done. So, issuing something the size of War and Peace full of 'therebys' and 'here-to-fores' is not necessarily a very helpful approach. Internally, we aim to use clear language and explanation, which does not have any legally binding powers but hopefully leads to understanding – surely the ultimate aim.

However, if your legal department insists on the use of a formal NDA rather than a simplified form, we would very heartily advise its pre-placement, by way of an attachment sent with the confirmation details that we issue to successfully recruited participants. That gives them the chance to print and read it at leisure, and we advise them that they must bring a signed copy with them on the day (or e-sign it back directly) or they will not be able to participate (and we reinforce this requirement when we make reminder calls).

Whilst we'd advise you to have a few printed copies on hand for any who forget, the point is that all have had time to read it and go through it before being asked to sign it, because no-one should be bounced into signing a legally binding document without that opportunity.

We've had negative feedback from participants hit with a huge contract on arrival, given barely time to skim it, and told they can't take part unless they get it signed before they leave reception, not even given a copy to keep – this puts really unfair pressure on them and often creates anxiety. This is definitely a Code of Conduct violation, because they feel worried and worse than before they took part and I think they'd have a pretty good defence legally as well, in the event of an accidental breach –they can't be bound by something signed under such pressure.

You also don't want your research time taken up with giving them the time it takes to read a legal document properly, or discussing the broader ramifications of clause 17. C (ii) …because there's always somebody. We can't make everyone read it of course, but we'll continue to stress the importance during recruitment – and advise that you continue to cover salient points during the introduction to your face-to-face research session.

We also talk about it again when we send our follow-up and thank-you emails, requesting them for their feedback. We remind them that they shouldn't tell us, or anybody, about anything that they were advised not to disclose during the session, such as the exact material they were shown. Just tell us in general terms how you felt about taking part.

Overkill? In the vast majority of cases, yes of course it is, but the point emphasises the prevention of a breach and understanding what one actually consists of.

We hope that everyone had a brilliant time taking part in your research event and will tell all their friends and family how good it was, and will be encouraged to register with Saros.

However, we don't want them to tell their friends exactly what the research was about. We can't police their private conversations but, nowadays, the conversation can be all too public. What used to go on privately in the office or bar now happens on Facebook or Tumblr, where far more people get to see it, (including potentially your client via their own routine social tracking).

One example we picked up from our own social media monitoring was a detailed and humorous blog post describing an experience attending a focus group on feminine hygiene products that the author had attended recently. We only noticed it because she mentioned Saros, and luckily it was simple enough to contact her and request that she kindly edit the piece and remove the reference to the brand involved, which she did very promptly. We had a good discussion about the issues involved, and she explained that she really hadn't understood what she could and couldn't say publicly.

She said it had been mentioned in the group but rather rushed over during the introductions, and she hadn't realised it applied to blogging as such. She thought we'd be glad she spread the word about taking part in research, and of course we were - but some specific references to a product and the way it was advertised had to be got rid of quickly.

This intelligent and articulate writer did not have a clear sense of what the limits were on what she could say, what was expected of her, at all. A written agreement could have prevented this from happening.

A second example, was when we heard from a client that a very detailed review of an unreleased software title of theirs, for which we'd recruited testers, had appeared online. They were, understandably, not happy. The review was so specific, down to iteration details, that we were able to identify the creator very easily simply from the dates involved – and whereas the blogger himself wasn't initially co-operative with our enquiries, his hosting company were far more understanding.

The offending content was removed within hours, and the NDA which he had signed did not have to be invoked legally. Had we not been able to help our client accomplish the take-down, there would have been recourse to escalate the matter legally however, because there was a specific agreement in place, which the participant had signed, and was legally bound by, despite his unhelpful reaction. He was just a young guy, full of enthusiasm about what had been revealed to him, and excited to have insider info on what was going on at a big gaming brand.

Incidentally, we do stress in our follow-up contact with all participants that whilst we hope they'll tell everyone how much they enjoyed being part of their project, to kindly remember that the content itself is confidential, the actual brands and things that they saw should not be mentioned.

This goes out a few days after their participation with their exit survey and, we hope, closes the loop …but it should be part of a process sealed with a legal document, if you are revealing anything sensitive, embargoed or controversial within the session itself, because there is very little leverage otherwise if someone decides to shout their mouth off.

Something we are happy to manage for you is pre-placement of your document and it doesn't need to be available to us for a few days after we have started recruitment. We will send it only after people are booked and confirmed into the session and we are sending their address and directions.

Your Criteria for Recruitment

Without a clear understanding of your desired recruitment criteria, we cannot even cost a project or discuss viability/timelines, never mind proceed to recruit it!

Essential vs Desirable recruitment criteria

The simplest way to present us with your recruitment criteria is in the form of a list of points, which describe your desired candidate, in terms of demographics, behaviour and attitude. To be honest, we'd prefer to work from that rather than reverse-engineer a telephone screener or pen-portrait, and it's the first thing we will try to distil your requirements down to before writing the screener which will capture whether a participant is a fit or not for your project.

Our intention is always to deliver on every single one of these points of course. That's what we set out to do, building a process on which to zero-in. However, on a complex recruit it can be particularly helpful to understand the respective importance of the different points, and how they relate to the research objectives behind them, if that is not immediately obvious.

This will help us create the screener (see below) to ensure we capture second-best options where appropriate or where there may be potential for flexibility should it be required later on in the process. Being clear about your absolute deal-breakers will make sure we don't come back with silly questions or ask you to consider accommodating someone who sounds like a good fit on most factors – but is an absolute no-no for reasons that might not be apparent because they haven't been shared with us. It also will stop us routing out and not even capturing the application of someone who might fail to fit on one factor, which could, on reflection, be open to debate.

Once again a great deal comes back to trusting your recruiter, with the holistic picture behind the research and the questions it is trying to answer, rather than just the narrowly defined recruitment spec. Please don't assume we will immediately disregard criteria revealed to us, as of secondary importance, as we don't work like that. Individuals are not personas and there may have to be a case of give and take to find the best fits.

Quota vs Spread

Qualitative research is not supposed to be demographically representative. It is intended, fully and fairly, to represent whatever segment of opinion you, the researcher, are keenest to explore.

Quite often in the list of recruitment criteria we will see a list of things like – 50/50 male/female, spread of ages from 20 to 45, half to be users of product X, remainder split between users of Y and Z, not more than 3 low users, minimum of A to be professional users and B lapsed users, and so on …lots of quite quantitative qualifiers describing the ideal breakdown of participants.

Now across a programme of 8 groups, we can write a plan to ensure we cover all of that swimmingly, and check every box, but when you write a spec in such granular detail for a day's user-testing involving 5 people, it all goes wrong. Our database is short on hermaphrodites and fractions of users for a start, and sometimes the maths simply doesn't work even in an ideal world.

Also, when there are 9 different interlocking quotas essential to the project, even with larger numbers, it can then be almost impossible to close the job. With 59 out of 60 people recruited we are now looking for the final person who has to be a male between 32 and 34 with a particular phone, occupation, usage level, postal sector and shoe-size. Heaven help us if anyone drops out and needs replacing, because the chances of having anyone who is going to slot in absolutely perfectly, at short notice, and fit all of that, is beyond possible.

Clearly, as with the essential vs desirable recruitment criteria, we may need to have a realistic dialogue about what aspects of achieving balance it makes sense to quota, and what elements we may respectfully suggest that you leave to us in order to achieve *spread*, rather than quota – such as, 'recruit a spread of people aged between 25 and 35'. If we are recruiting 60 people we'd expect to see a pretty even distribution of most of each age in that decade, but if we are recruiting 6 we will aim to have 20s and 30s fairly evenly split and the extremes of the range represented as best we can – as it falls out, within all the other factors that go into choosing the best possible participants for your project.

When it comes to brand usage, split of users vs. rejecters and similar factors, then absolutely let's put hard quotas on it – that is what your research is all about, the factors you want to control and compare directly. That's fine, but when it comes to the demographics, please do consider trusting us to achieve a representative spread within your chosen parameters, without feeling the need to set quotas on every attribute from IQ to underwear size.

Because qual is not quant, recruitment is an art not a science, and human beings are not personas.

It all comes down to dialogue and openness, and making sure we ask you the right questions to ensure we completely understand your priorities and will get the best possible fit for your project – all the more important if numbers are particularly low.

Defining Behaviours

With everything said above in respect to quotas on demographics, we accept that your client has specific knowledge, when it comes to who their customers are. They know who they want to research and roughly what that person is going to look like, behave like and so on.

However, this goes back to the question of essential vs desirable criteria, because in recruitment we encounter real people, and they don't always fit the lovingly-crafted personas and pen-portraits generated by the previous research exercise (especially if that turns out to be a quant study 20 years ago, as we have occasionally encountered).

We would suggest, on any potentially complex or problematic recruit, focusing first on the brand-related behaviour that you are primarily seeking to explore. If it turns out that the people fitting this are in fact skewing lower in age than expected, for example, we can discuss this as it arises – it might be that you can regard it as a finding, that it re-shapes some of the intended direction of the research, because usage patterns are not as expected.

It could be there is something in the way the questions are written which is biasing the response and we need to tweak that, as the recruit unfolds. Either way, if we only invite applications from people in a very narrowly-defined age-band, we won't find that out during recruitment.

There might be other reasons why the answers aren't reflecting the behaviour your hard data suggests should be the case. A great deal comes down to how something is phrased, but even with extreme care in screener creation, there are all sorts of trends and social factors.

We recruited a successful round of research for a vintner, wanting to import new wines to the UK, and particularly keen to talk to regular drinkers of dry rosé wines. No problem, great groups, everybody happy. They were so happy in fact, that they decided to run some more groups a few months later, and suddenly the incidence was much lower... We were using an almost identical screener, but the outcomes were completely different.

Puzzled, we called back some of the people who had screened in previously, to talk to them about the project as a quality-control measure. It was months later but, of course, they remembered taking part. So, do they still drink rosé? *"Well no not now – it's November! That's my summer drink!"*

What happened was we were using a screener asking about preferences, likes and dislikes, whereas what we should have been asking about was actual behaviour. *"How frequently do you drink?"* not, *"Which are your favourite drinks?"* It had worked out fine in the summer, because they were all sitting in riverside pubs sipping chilled rosé and described it as a favourite, quite accurately, because that was how they felt about it, but we didn't factor in the idea that it was now cold and dark outside and a nice hearty red probably went down rather better on most evenings these days.

Even behavioural questions would have to factor in

seasonal factors like this.

In fact, we are all quite poor witnesses to our own intentions and preferences. We are much better at being honest and accountable about what we actually DID, rather than what we think, believe, or expect. So we try to write screener questions about actual behaviour, instead of anything else. What was the last brand of shampoo that you bought – which do you buy most often – not, which do you like best? This is further complicated of course when we are asking about behaviour that might seem less desirable or aspirational, things that people may feel conflicted or uncomfortable about, or in straightforward denial. We can use neutral, non-rejecting language, but consider, if you will, recruiting – something that is simply regarded as socially invisible or unacceptable, perhaps, to certain segments of the population.

We once had a project, for an underwriter, where we needed to recruit people who regarded themselves as below-averagely competent car drivers. One hates to reinforce a stereotype, but let's just say the women's group filled up fairly easily, but try finding 9 men who a) regard themselves as poorer drivers, and b) actually want to come and discuss that fact in a group of other men... We actually joked that we had to send fewer invites to recruit on the project for erectile dysfunction in the same quarter, (not to draw any conclusions regarding comparative incidence or correlation...)

Anything to do with weight and dieting is tricky. No point asking if people want to eat more healthily or could do with losing some weight, because very few are going to disagree with that – but if you ask about weight and height, with dress size as sense check, you can work out who is eligible for a group about weight loss products. We also have to bear in mind that in most recruits, more people are going to screen out as ineligible than get recruited – and we won't be able to tell them why.

Of course, screening on attitude is essential in qualitative recruitment, and there are ways and means to make sure that it is done both sensitively and robustly. We'll cover that in detail in the next chapter, but where we can focus a question on what people do instead of why, that tends to make for more effective screening, at least at the initial question and response stage. The 'why?' may be far more interesting in the long run, but then that's your job in the event itself.

Working with Your Recruiter

Contact and Availability

As discussed above, the briefing of a job is a critical time, and we pay a lot of attention to making sure it goes right – everybody clear on what the recruitment criteria are, what screening questions will be used, the schedule and logistics and so on. Hopefully we all leave that call knowing exactly what is required of us, and we can go on and get started on your recruit without further delays.

However, recruitment is not a linear, scientific process; there can be quirks and unexpected things can happen along the way. Whilst appreciating the implicit trust, it is very difficult to work effectively with a client who drops a brief on us then goes away for a fortnight's holiday without leaving us a contact point. This has happened on more than one occasion, a quick query pings an 'Out of Office' autoresponder and we are left in a vacuum having to make decisions on a recruit which should be referred outwith the recruiter level. We're quite capable of making a judgement call where appropriate, but if there are serious issues with the screener or the location of a venue and we are not in direct contact with your client, we need urgent access to somebody on your team during the whole recruitment process to avoid wasting precious recruitment time, trying to work out who to talk to.

Other times, of course, researchers want to be far more heavily involved, and that's fine too. We actually want you to sign off the screener and our project spec. If you are around we'd like to give you regular updates as well, talk to you about anything unusual that may come up in recruitment - but that's a bare minimum involvement, far from the only possible arrangement.

We have clients who actually like to do the shortlisting for callback alongside us, and that's fine too, in fact it can work really well. Particularly for a more exploratory kind of screener with lots of open-ended questions maybe leading to a more ethnographic style of project, it can be really valuable for you to review the responses received and see who leaps out as being exactly who you want to talk to in the end. It might end up not being the people you originally specified, or that we thought you wanted - but who knows what kind of magic a good open-ended question or two might elicit, that takes things off in a unexpected direction.

Working in this way, the recruitment itself becomes a truly qualitative process.

Other clients might want to make the final decision about the composition of the groups, once initial responses are in. Treating the data almost quantitatively at this point, we are happy to strip out the sensitive/contact info and send it over so you can have a look and see... *Hmm, greater proportion of lapsed users than we had considered and they are clustering in the second location. Let's do an extra mini group there to explore the reason for this, or revise the split between the users and non-user groups in that area to look at it more closely.*

We can even sort the data for you into batches and tabs - we're not statisticians, but our Research Bookers are a whizz at wrangling spreadsheets and sorting responses every which way you could imagine, they have to do that before picking up the phone.

We'd much rather take the time to ensure we focus on calling the people who are the best possible fit, than present you with profiles that aren't quite what you imagined later on in the process.

The only thing about this approach is that, of course, it takes time - and this has to be added to the existing stated timelines for the project as a whole. If there is no activity built into the recruitment plan to cover *'researcher sits on responses for 3 days before telling us who we can call'* then that time is lost to us, when we should be working on the interviewing and getting people confirmed into the job.

We are totally happy to take the recruitment criteria, have you sign off the screener and spec, and then not bother you again until the project is full… So long as, as indicated above, we are able to reach you in the event of any queries or matters arising.

But if you would like to get more hands-on, let's get that clear at the start, and we'll make a plan that involves regular collaboration and contact.

Incidentally when we do send those final profiles, usually a couple of days before the group, please do review them promptly. It's not impossible to find out that something has gone wrong or is simply unexpected at that point - for example, on occasion a change of venue has not been relayed to us, or an incorrect date gets approved.

Two or three days before the fieldwork starts, we have a good chance of correcting this and wrestling the project back on track, but if you leave the email unopened until you are on your way to the viewing facility, that is a very bad time to find out anything is not precisely as expected.

The Recruitment Screener

In almost all cases where a project has not gone to plan, or not produced the result a client was hoping for, we can generally isolate the problem back to one place: the screener. Getting this document right is the foundation for the entire recruitment effort, because everything else we do – the telephone interview, preparation of profiles etc. – all spin off from this. We need to make sure we work together and cover everything carefully.

The Role of the Screener in Participant Recruitment.

Having explained everything above, regarding the importance of the screener it is necessary to recognise its specific role in the recruitment process –not the recruitment process itself perhaps, but rather as crucial element within it.

Screeners are used differently under different models of recruitment, but in our case what we describe as the screener is the initial online questionnaire, by which we invite our pre-selected members in order that they can express interest or otherwise in the project as a whole. Our intentions then, in writing this questionnaire, are:

1. To tell potential participants a bit about the research, approximately when and where it's taking place, how long it is, the incentive on offer and, roughly, what it's all about – to enable them to make an informed decision about whether they are interested and available to participate.

2. To confirm and double-check certain bits of information about them, already known to us from their entry on our database. (This is also triple-checked on the phone). All will have been pre-selected to receive the invitation based on information they previously shared with us, but such information can change over time. People Sometimes change jobs or have a baby and, unthinkable as it sounds, they neglect to update their Saros profile immediately, so we cover all that again in the screener, even if we are expecting everybody to give the same answer.

3. To elicit screening data uniquely applicable to the project in hand – all of which will, again, be checked by telephone. This is where we get into the nitty gritty of who is going to be eligible to participate in your project, and our intention is to cover all the factual elements that could potentially rule them in, or out, of your project. This means that when our interviewer talks to them, they are not wasting either party's time having conversations with people who are definitely not eligible, or not free on Thursday evening.

Of course, people do screen out on the phone for various reasons, not least because we check all the questionnaire responses again. It's usually a few days later on, and we find that people occasionally change their answers. The reasons for this are various, it could be anything from a simple mis-click to a deliberate lie or attempt to second-guess the criteria. They might simply feel differently on a different day... This can easily happen with attitudinal questions, but it can also happen with product-behaviour questions in categories about which they don't care deeply or buy without thinking.

If asked to name the brand of kitchen roll you last bought, would you remember? If asked again a few days later, you might well say something different.

Generally, the screener will capture what we are looking for in terms of facts and the interviewer can go through those fairly quickly by phone given that most are consistent, overall, in their responses. This means they are free to focus on the softer qualities that define an effective, and hopefully excellent, participant... Are they enthusiastic enough about the category to be able to engage with it for a two-hour group discussion? Especially if it's about kitchen roll. Are they sufficiently articulate and conversational? Do they have a voice and accent clear enough to be understood in a group, or would they be better being tagged as preferred for one-to-one projects instead? Can they use their imagination to answer spontaneous questions creatively but appropriately?

They're also focussed on whether or not they actually seem committed to taking part. The fact that people sometimes make multiple-project applications before being successfully recruited by us, can work in favour of that, to actually 'get the call' – some people act as if they had just won a sweepstake, but anybody who appears to be hesitant about their diary or simply implies that they're doing a favour, won't get booked in. We know they're the weak link, likely to *'no-show'* or cancel late, and it's just not going to stick. *Next!*

The best screener in the world cannot make any of those judgements, the human input is essential in every aspect of qual, but what the screener can do is make sure the humans speak to the right candidates, and focus their effort and time on those most likely to yield a successful recruit.

Another thing the screener is NOT, incidentally, is a data-collection exercise.

While quite reasonable to collect information in a range not directly related to eligibility for the purposes of blind recruiting – about the purchasing frequency of 5 different kinds of shampoo, for example, to hide the one we care about. Such data isn't part of the recruitment process and will not be included for those ones who screen into the project who, in any case, are likely to be very low fraction of those completing the screener.

If you want quantitative data about shampoo usage collected on the back of the screener, and you want the data from all of the responses as well as the 16 you end up meeting face to face, that is fine – but we owe it to our members to be transparent about this fact, and to reward them all for taking part. A prize draw for unsuccessful applicants is fine – and acknowledges that they have contributed to a process in exchange for something, even if it's not the opportunity to take part in the face-to-face stage of the project.

This is important because our relationship with

members is based on trust. Some of them spend what probably adds up to hours of their life completing our screeners over months, until we finally find the job with their name on. They need to be able to trust us that the time is spent solely for a shot at the paying project, that their responses are not being monetised by us or anyone else for other purposes – so we will always require clarity on this fact at the outset.

Who Writes the Screener?

"But we've already got a screener!" I hear you cry!

Brilliant! That is a huge help to us, because we will be able to use your exact wording to generate our own, and ensure a precise match – particularly important when you are comparing results across different markets or over different timespans.

However, it's unlikely we will be able to use it, in the exact form in which you hand it over to us. We will, in fact, end up having actually to reverse-engineer it to fit our unique processes. For example, the first thing we'll do is extract the demographic questions, excluded occupations, and anything else we can use in our pre-selection process, when we search our database to long-list possibilities. Where possible, we only post invitations to people who are already pre-screened on whatever we can up-front (even though it gets rechecked as indicated above) – this helps target the people most likely to be responsive and avoids wasting other people's time – and also offers your client some protection against those within the same industry becoming aware of the research.

We'll use a lot of the questions you give us, word-for-word, in our online screener of course – although, occasionally, things have to be adapted slightly for use online, rather than on the phone or street, if that is what they were originally designed for. Sometimes there are cultural or interpretation issues we have to review to fit the UK market, and we'll discuss with you anything that doesn't make sense or seems to have been lost in translation along the way. Dare we say it, not every question in every screener always appears to have been written by a logically-minded native English speaker, and we can review that as we go along.

Half-hour screeners do not get meaningful numbers of applicants, so we sometimes find that, for clarity and speed of completion, questions can be condensed or combined. Sometimes they make better sense if reordered as well. You will always be able to review any proposed changes and happy to explain the thinking behind them, which is based on experience in preparing many similar documents.

For example, we have occasionally been sent a screener that makes it abundantly clear which one is the client's preferred product, even though we have been instructed to blind this during recruitment. There might be a previous question asking about 5 brands of shampoo, but if this is followed by, *"What do you like most about Brand X?",* then it's not going to stay very well-blinded, nor is it neutral. So we'll make changes that support the objectives of the exercise as a whole, which is to capture Brand X loyalists/preferrers, but without making it hopelessly obvious that they're the only ones going through... Because if they say to our interviewer - or your moderator - *"This is about Brand X, isn't it?"* we all look like fools.

Of course whilst a pre-written screener, on which we can paste useful chunks, is a great help to us, we are also quite happy to work without one, and it's part of our professional service to develop all the materials needed during the recruit. If your criteria are listed in bullet points (preferred) or embedded in a persona or pen-portrait, we can work with that. If they're all in your head it's trickier but, if you prefer, we can take your briefing over the phone then email it back to you for checking – it only becomes a problem if it stays in your head and doesn't get shared with us, Crucial criteria revealed once the recruit is well underway, can poke spectacular holes in a watertight process.

Indeed, for all the reasons we will discuss below in the section on creating good screeners, we do need to have all the recruitment criteria and eligibility factors in front of us from the outset. It can be exceptionally difficult to crowbar additional factors in afterwards, even if the recruitment hasn't started. If at all possible, please let's get the screening criteria fully agreed between both parties before we proceed to create the questionnaire itself, because how we structure this and order the questions, depends on the whole thing, and late changes might create considerable additional work.

We then just need to focus on making sure we create a really good screener, which meets all of our mutual objectives. We will code this up and then send you a link to inspect it, along with a description of any routing or back-coding, not immediately obvious, because once the screener is complete, we will require you to review and sign it off before we deploy it. In this way we can be certain we are all working from an agreed starting point, that will ultimately go on to deliver the right participants for your event. Once the screener is signed off, it is likely that any further changes might affect costs and deliverability.

The importance of this screener is beyond doubt. how can we help make sure that between us we create a good screener, the best possible? Simply stated, a good screener is comprised of good questions, asked in the right way, and arranged in the right order.

Whether you or we are writing the screener, or it is a

combination of the two, these are the principles by which we strive to come up with a final questionnaire that works and gets the results we need.

Writing good screening questions

A good screening question to use in qualitative research recruitment will have to pass a number of tests. Some of these are simply common sense, others are subtler, and not every criterion will apply to every kind of question but, overall, a good question for a screener will meet the following conditions:

1. It's directly aligned with the required information the answer will yield.

For example, don't ask about their assessment with a support representative's skill level, if what you really want to know is, *"How satisfied were you with the service you received?"*. If you need to know whether they eat chocolate at home at least once a week, don't ask a complicated question about all the different settings in which chocolate could be eaten. There is no commercial sensitivity involved in blinding the home location, and no indication of which is the right or wrong answer – why not simply ask how often they eat chocolate at home? This is one reason why starting with a list of bullet points as the recruitment criteria makes a great deal of sense.

You can ensure that each bullet point is covered with a question, that matches the kind of response needed, rather than confusing it.

2. It is written clearly and unambiguously

To write questions clearly, you have to imagine yourself into the mind of the respondent, and their potential lack of any background whatsoever in either your product, your research objectives, or your professional experience.

It has been proven that it actually creates discomfort for respondents, if they have to guess or extrapolate, or feel torn between different responses because the instruction is not clear.

It certainly cannot make for good screening. So, it is essential to use clear instruction. If you are referring to measurements or time periods, be precise.

Make sure you are truly only asking one question at a time – because they can only give one answer in a closed response system. *"Do you agree that the representative who called you was knowledgeable and courteous?"* should be two questions with separate answers, which might not be the same. Ask yourself, almost to the point of absurdity, could the wording in this question possibly be misinterpreted or misunderstood? *"How long did you expect the pizza to be?"* *"Well I expected it to be about 12 inches across..."*

Do not ask respondents to decide for themselves what you mean by a word. For example, often questions are written with a list of closed responses along the lines of 'very frequently' 'somewhat frequently', etc. but what does the word 'frequently' actually mean? It can mean different things to different people in different circumstances.

Try to avoid the use of highly subjective words like 'regularly', 'usually', 'frequently', 'typically', together, particularly in ratings scales. Why not simply use a scale of one to 5 instead? Even in simple yes/no questions, it's ambiguous. *"Do you regularly drink vintage champagne?"* might be answered *"No"* because you're a daily drinker of non-vintage fizz, only breaking out the expensive stuff at weekends ...but another respondent might think, *"Well, we have our favourite wedding champagne every year on our anniversary, so I definitely drink it regularly, like clockwork."* Completely different behaviours, which should not screen into the same group discussion.

Similarly, avoid words like 'manage' or 'handle' – because these two are more subjective than might first appear.

"Who handles your IT support?"

"Well ...there's the smart girl in the office we always ask if we can't do something in Excel – ...there's the guys downstairs we ring if the screen goes blue – and there is an external consultant we call if we can't connect to the main server."

So what is the answer to this question? Perhaps it's the same people who 'handle' our phone contracts, but I have to 'handle' the phone every time I pick it up to call them – lack of clarity will create inconsistent responses.

Reading your question aloud as if you were speaking to somebody directly, is often a good way of making sure it is clear and makes sense. Above all write your question in a natural language, keeping it as short as you possibly can – but no shorter.

3. It uses words and phrases that participants themselves might use and understand, which are both neutral and globally applicable

This is important, particularly if the research itself is about something technical or specialist. So if we're recruiting for a medical project, we want to use the terms that the patients themselves would use to describe the condition rather than those that doctors would use. They have been diagnosed with hypertension, but would be more likely to describe themselves as suffering from high blood pressure. People buy fresh fruit and vegetables rather than produce, sweets and snacks rather than confectionery. Nobody shops for FMCG! Basically, all industry jargon acronyms and the like should be reframed from the participants' point of view. This is one of the most frequent bits of editing we have to apply to otherwise well-written screeners that are presented to us.

It can also mean applying thoughtful culturally specific translations to international documents as well. We have had great confusion in questions from the US referring to 'holidays' – but they weren't talking about vacations, they were talking about what in the UK we call Christmas, which completely altered the meaning and understanding of the question.

Other times, the question might be written from the point of view of one brand or manufacturer, and simply not applicable to the competitors they also want to recruit. An advanced iOS user would be unlikely to describe themselves as likely to root their phone, whereas they're quite likely to jailbreak it. It can occasionally be difficult letting a client know that the terminology is not universally understood, but we do have to make sure screening language is accessible to everybody we might need to recruit.

This is in no way to patronise respondents or to make assumptions about their intelligence or their reading level, incidentally. It is simply about ensuring that as many people as possible respond fully and accurately to the written screener, so that we are able to find the best matches in recruitment.

4. It is easy to answer - people are likely to know or remember what the correct answer is.

"How many times has you visited your general practitioner within the last five years?"

Whilst these questions may be asked to try and get an overview of behaviour over time and in order to overcome blips – for example, briefly acute periods of illness – it's actually going to be somewhat of a guess for almost all participants.

It would surely make more sense to ask them about visits within the past six or 12 months, and a separate question about how many of these were for distinct reasons. Guesses won't help us recruit the people you need, and remember that it also creates feelings of discomfort in the participants themselves if they sense that their answers might be inaccurate or made-up.

This affects completion rate, and also how they feel about the whole project, how they will feel about clicking through to the next screen questionnaire if they don't get selected for this one…

Questions asking people either to remember a long way back, or to perform arithmetical calculations are often simply more demanding then they need to be.

If you ask people what percentage of their work time they spend doing a particular activity, they might not even do the maths right, even if they estimate it correctly in the first place.

Easier to simply ask them to rank activities in order of proportion of time taken, or ask about a specific example day in the recent past. You could also use a time-based yardstick such as, *"On your last 10 trips to the doctor, how frequently did you have your medication reviewed?"* –

Rather than ask them on what percentage or proportion of visits their prescription was updated, raising the stakes about the level of accuracy expected.

Often questions can be made easier to answer by including just a few extra qualifying words or terms.

For example, by adding a timeframe – *"How often did you visit the supermarket* in the past two weeks?" Is simply much easier to answer than, *"How often do you visit the supermarket?"*

If you really need to ask the question that respondents might not be able to answer with accuracy, such as one which requires recall of events long-past, then you can acknowledge this in the wording. Give them permission to be vague or have a guess.

"How old were you approximately when you first experienced your IBS symptoms?"

If you don't include a qualifier, people might agonise about exactly when it first happened… perhaps it was years ago, perhaps they just not sure when they first noticed the symptoms. Or do they mean when first diagnosed?

Perhaps I should come back and fill this thing in later once I have given it a bit more thought, or even checked with my consultant…

If you are writing a closed response question, you can give the participants a helpful indicator of detail required, by the way you group your responses together. In the previous example, you could offer a drop-down list of diagnosed before age 10, diagnosed during teens, during your 20s etc.

This immediately removes any pressure for them to be accurate and, hopefully, maps nicely onto your quotas for the recruitment anyway

5. It offers a complete universe of closed responses

If a question requires an answer, but the respondent feels that no answer particularly fits for them, what are they supposed to do? It is likely that people will try to guess or make up a response when they simply don't have one to give, and thereby reducing the likelihood of good screening.

Avoiding this problem is very often as simple as including options such as 'not applicable' or 'other'.

Of course, you might wish to avoid this on attitudinal questions – where you really want to know what a participant thinks – even encourage them TO think – not to let them off the hook for having no opinion.

In this case, you would want to use a rating scale with no middle option, forcing them to come down slightly in one direction or another...

However, when it comes to giving an opinion on a service or product they have not used, it's important to give them the option of simply declining to answer.

At other times, failing to include enough options might simply make people question their own behaviour. If asked about frequency of visits to the dentist, and the responses range from within the last month to within the last year, what about the people who never or almost never go near a dentist for whatever reason? This hasn't captured the complete range of possible responses, so even if such a response is of no interest to you from a recruitment perspective, you must include 'less often' in the possibilities. (You could also offer 'never', but this should be in addition to 'less often' – because otherwise the person who hasn't filed up for an examination for five years cannot respond accurately).

Sometimes there are issues here too, of sensitivity and correctness.

For example, if you are only interested in people with a high household income, you don't want to offer too many options amongst the lower income brackets – however if you have a question with a menu saying under £50,000, £50,000-£65,000, £65,001-£80,000 and so on, this might well make people with a wide range of respectable mid to low incomes feel a little bit dismissed and uncomfortable when completing it.

Even if they are an automatic screen out for the project in hand, it is more respectful to offer people the chance to answer as though their information matters, and include a range of lower income bracket options – just because it doesn't matter to you for this project, it matters to them.

6. Do not point to the desired/required answer

It is a sad fact that, because cash incentives are on offer, there are people who will try to be less than truthful in their applications to take part in qualitative research.

They will try to guess what makes a 'successful' application, and work out what it is that the researcher is looking for.

After all, we do our best to make the prospect of selection as attractive and enticing as we can.

However much we say that they cannot know what the correct response is – please just be honest, spontaneous and genuine – we know that a number of factors come into play ...from social-desirability, people-pleasing, to outright attempts to second-guess the system.

Of course, this is usually very obvious in an application that appears utterly unfocused and agrees with everything, often contradicts itself in different questions, and so on.

Our interviewers tend to spot these a mile off and not call them anyway, but when writing the questions in the first place, it is obviously essential to avoid leading participants to what we are looking for.

Do you have a pay-as-you-go mobile phone?

Answer: yes or no.

Obviously then, participants realise this is exactly what we are looking for, and it will affect their response not only to this question but all of the subsequent ones – *Hmm ...they only want pay-as-you-go customers ...perhaps they are looking for people with certain handsets, or maybe with certain lifestyles or incomes.*

Of course, we cannot stop people speculating as they will, however much content we generate the need to 'be yourself' and 'be a complete whole person', and the importance of waiting 'til the perfect match project comes up, etc.

We can avoid introducing clear signals like this in the screening questionnaire by simply asking a neutral question:

Is your mobile phone

a) on a prepaid contract; or b) pay-as-you-go?

On longer lists we'll work to avoid order bias, including techniques such as randomising or alphabetising the list of responses.

Whilst it will never be possible to hide the fact that we are interested in different kinds of phone contracts – and why would we? – We can always find a way to phrase a question so that it does not point people straight at the 'hoped for' answer.

7. Are neutral, fair and unbiased

Research for any purpose means asking questions and eliciting responses in a way that does not influence those responses. Other areas of the MRS Code of Conduct, which don't concern themselves directly with participant welfare, are very much about the quality and integrity of the research itself.

Qualitative recruitment is part of an overall research exercise, which must generate reliable and consistent results, not those that are steered or distorted by the design of the project itself. It's important to pay attention to the use of value-laden and loaded terms and phrases that might creep into screening questions.

After all, language itself is culturally constructed and simply not neutral. We use words as a tool to probe thoughts and behaviours and, as such, we have a duty to make sure those words are as balanced as possible. This can be particularly important in questions about attitude or socio-political matters: *"Are you in favour of a tax on fat-cat executives?"* creates an immediate negative loading, segregating those nasty fat-cats, and encouraging the response, *"Hell yes, let's fleece them of their ill-gotten gains!"* Asking instead about taxes on high-earners, or defining those high-earners in terms of annual income, is much more factual and neutral and will allow the respondent to consider their reply less emotionally.

When some degree of loading is inevitable, we simply have to try to make it fair and equal. for example, *"Which of these factors do you consider to be the greatest contributor to global warming? Steady consumption of fossil fuels by developed nations or excessive demands caused by growth of emergent markets?"*

Removal of the value-judgemental words 'excessive' and 'steady' would rebalance this question more effectively, because they contain the implication that one is predictable, allowable and consistent while the other is over-the-top and unnecessary, which cannot but have an influence on the people answering the question.

Bias can come into it too. From the participant's point of view, psychology informs that – all things being equal, most of us prefer to agree rather than disagree. We want to be agreeable people we also want to be selected for what we hope is a paid face-to-face research event… So, if we are asked – *"Are you aware of any advertising of discount travel for students?"* – there is a definite inclination for more people to answer *"yes"*, than are actually aware of said advertising.

One way around this can be to include an option like, 'don't know' or 'not sure', but biases like this we simply have to accept as part of human nature.

Asking about other advertising they might have spotted for other markets, of course, gives them more options to agree or disagree, rather than feeling it hangs on one question.

This is one more reason for the thorough telephone interviews we conduct with all applicants before recruiting them into a qualitative event; talking to them directly we can ask what they recall about this advertising, what it looked like, where they saw and heard it – and they will have to give a spontaneous and un-googled reply.

Making the decision about whether or not to book them into the group is a qualitative one, using data gleaned from the more quantitative screener submission, in combination with human factors such as listening and instinct.

Writing screening questions will always be an art rather

than a science, one dependent on the delightful fluctuations of human behaviour in all its diversity. But that's the reason you do research in the first place isn't it?

Planning and compiling the screener

As well as having a great selection of carefully written screen questions, we also need to put them together in a single screening questionnaire, which will be the top of the funnel for recruiting your qualitative or user-experience participants.

One important thing to consider is the overall hierarchy and flow. Whether your questionnaire follows a routing pathway or is all effectively on a single page, it only makes sense to ask questions from a broad perspective through to a tight one.

For example, in a screener about usage of hair conditioner, we might ask first, 'which of the following personal care products do you use at least twice a week?' Then go on to ask about their preferred brands of conditioner, if they use it, and when they buy it. It would look completely random and silly to do it the other way round, to ask them where they shop for a product and then ask whether or not they use it.

Grouping questions together also makes sense, because although any one screener should really all be about the same subject, there might be different kinds or categories of questions you are asking about it. In our conditioner example, there might be a segment of the questionnaire dealing specifically with brand usage and frequency, then there might be a bunch of questions about packaging and displays, another one about attitudes to product ingredients, presentation and animal testing, and so on.

If these are grouped together it is helpful to the participant, and even more so if a little bit of transitional text is included to signify a shift of direction: *"Now we're going to ask you a few 'attitude' questions about your choice of personal care products in general"*.

We use this kind of transitional label to isolate other important bits of the screening questionnaire, such as their availability for the different time slots and contact information so that our interviewer can reach them within the next few days.

The overall length of the screener is important. It matters both how long the questionnaire looks on the page and how long it will take them to fill it in.

As previously discussed, it is important to bear in mind that this is not a quantitative survey that participants are completing for its own sake or reward – for them it is purely the first step in, hopefully, being accepted into a paid research event. They are not rewarded for their time in any way, and it is not fair to use this time to collect anything beyond direct eligibility criteria.

If additional information is required in profiling the candidates, but doesn't affect their eligibility, this can be collected later on the phone.

Rather than the number of questions or responses required, the most important thing overall is how long it takes to complete the screener. This has a huge impact on the number of submissions we receive, and that of course directly impacts on the quality of recruit we can perform for you.

Exactly how many long-listed candidates we invite to apply for your event depends on a great many different factors, including the simple incidence of your qualifying criteria, what we know about the responsiveness of that demographic segment, and our potential overall timelines in terms of sending further waves of invitations.

However, with a well written and tight screener at the end of the link, we are able to make reasonably reliable assumptions about how many responses we're likely to receive over a 24-hour period from the initial invitation. Deviation from this is generally down to a screener that people simply give up on.

Our click-through rates from our invitation emails to the questionnaire itself are relatively consistent, but when they reach the questionnaire, if they get stuck, bored, frustrated or otherwise distracted, then we've lost that response.

Huge grid questions, exhorting them to compare or rate 20 different products on a scale of seven or more different factors, might be a single question that takes ages and ages to complete properly – and of course we can tell very easily if they became fed up and just started 'satisficing' their way through by clicking down the middle responses.

Of course you want to obscure which product most interests you, but do you really need 19 dummy items? Are there better ways of soliciting the same information, such as by combining questions that ask almost the same thing? A single closed-response question might well be answered in a few seconds – or it might require a great deal of thought, depending on the question.

Similarly, an open-ended question might require the typing of the single word, or somebody might put great time and effort into writing a fuller response, perhaps awkwardly on a small touchscreen device.

More factors than might first be apparent go into determining the length of time it takes to complete a screener …which is not to say the visual appearance on the page isn't also important.

Because appearance matters, we do our best to ensure our screeners look consistent, as well as visually appealing. We make use of images where appropriate, and in the unusual event where a recruit can be completely unblinded we are happy to co-brand our screeners with your logo or that of your client.

We can also incorporate pack shots of your product if name recall is likely to be challenging, although bear in mind that for the sake of blind recruitment we will also need to get hold of similar pack shots for the competitor brands.

Although we don't want to make the questionnaire pages longer than they need to be or take longer to load on the participants' devices, we will always work to ensure an appealing and attractive visual appearance which is likely to encourage people to carry on and answer all the questions to apply successfully.

We will even occasionally use video in our screeners, but we're more likely to do this where there is a complex methodology to explain, rather than as part of a question, particularly if this is combined with trying to attract an audience who might be less inclined to read detailed paragraphs of explanation.

Combined with a logically designed screener containing carefully written questions, we can hopefully reduce the most bewilderingly convoluted project down to a screener that works, and get us the right people to interview for your research project.

Screening for imagination, creativity and articulateness

As well as ensuring that participants meet your recruitment criteria from a factual and attitudinal point of view, and ensuring they are committed and capable of attending your session, it is often important to ensure we test their powers of imagination and creativity.

They could be a perfect fit for your group in every way, but the last thing you want is to have somebody sitting there contributing nothing – just because they are unable to make the mental connections between their own thoughts and life experiences, and the stimulus material shared with them. People think and express themselves in widely different ways, some of which make for great research participation, others less so. Some are more necessary when participating in a group session, where others may have specific attributes that makes them ideal for a one to one in-depth conversation

Depending on what you tell us about your research activity, we will test participants' powers of imagination in a range of different ways. This will generally be done during the telephone selection process, rather than as part of the online screener. We do not want somebody googling the answers to a creativity question, or spending hours crafting the perfect response... Instead we want to know whether they are capable of thinking and coming up with ideas spontaneously, in the moment – just as they might be expected to do during the session itself.

Word-association is a good way to test their command of language, and ability to link concepts together. It is a particularly strong indicator of a participant who will contribute well in a branding exercise, anything to do with naming products, or developing slogans and strap-lines.

If you have a particular workshop requiring these skills in above-average depth, of course we can always look for other good indicators, such as an interest in language – reading and writing – generally, or people with a passion for word games, crosswords and scrabble. We once recruited a Countdown finalist for a product naming workshop – but from his civil service occupation you'd never have guessed his hidden passion for words and having fun with them, which brought great insight to the project in hand.

You might require a more visual imagination if you are developing logos and brand graphics, or perhaps at other times if you are conducting a tracking study looking at changes in a brand over time. You might need people who are more than averagely attuned to the subtle differences a rebranding can indicate, and remembering particular things about colours and shapes. We would ask different kinds of questions to identify people who would contribute well to this kind of research. They would not necessarily be the kind of people who would describe themselves as artistic, nor need they have any kind of professional background in design related matters – but we look for people who have enthusiasms about visual things from fashion to photography, can talk about what they like to see in different things, what things symbolise to them, and why.

If you are having to show quite early stage conceptual work to research participants, such as the wireframes or diagrams instead of a website, illustrations and projections instead of a physical product, then a different kind of imagination is required.

You need people who can make a leap in space and time, join the dots to create something new, and see the future as you have envisaged it in your development process. The same kinds of thinkers are often great at packaging design research, because they have a way of visualising things in motion and three-dimensional from descriptions and photographs.

People who like working with their hands, who have tactile, craft-hobbies, can be good indicators for this, but we also have specific questions designed to draw out the imaginations of any potential applicant, whether they are currently expressing this side of themselves through their work and hobbies or not. And we can look for specific evidence of creativity associated with them online, such as Pinterest boards or involvement in prosumer/maker forums.

Even things like the good old favourite, "Tell me six things you can do with a brick, other than build with it", tells you a great deal about how people's minds work, what style of thinking they employ by default, and also how they respond, under pressure, to be creative on demand. We know a telephone selection interview is not the same as being in a room with strangers, but there they will have the synergy of the group and visual stimulus as well.

If they can free-associate well and creatively with our interviewer, there is a good chance they will contribute effectively in the room, and this kind of question also occasionally helps to weed out somebody who is thinking is really rather warped or strange. A candidate once told our interviewer that the first five things he associated with the colour green were all different kinds of agricultural equipment – mostly tractor parts, which he named and referenced by manufacturer and serial number. He never made it to the group discussion, but I guess he would have been great in the right pub quiz...

For special unique projects we have occasionally built unique screening questions, in liaison with our clients. One researcher needed to talk to people with synaesthesia, unusual connections between the senses. If you don't know what colour the number 7 is, or can't describe what a symphony tastes like, then this would not have been the right project for you, it wasn't for most participants particularly as very specific synaesthetes were required, but I would have loved to observe that session when they got together.

Unless you have something specific in mind, we will choose suitable imagination-challenging questions to use as part of our telephone interviewing process, based, in general, on that which we know will work, and also what we know about the types of skills and activities that will be involved on the night.

This is another reason why it is a great help to us to know about the kinds of exercises you will be employing in the session, the kind of thinking that you will be needing. We don't need to see your discussion guide, or know anything confidential about what exactly you would talk to them in the research, but if you can share with us some background as to the kind of projective techniques you use, this really helps us to screen participants most effectively for you.

One approach we might take with you is discussing your ideal candidate, and what you hoped they would bring to the project. What kind of person would they be? – In conversation, what would they be like? The way you describe them will help us to identify the kind of thinking that could distinguish a really great participant from an okay one.

The vegetarian fried chicken loyalist

A final point on screener creation, is the importance of defining screen-out criteria.

The title is a real example, from a fast food focus group we once recruited. We didn't know that the client was pretty much defined by their fried chicken product, because we didn't know who the end client was, and we dutifully recruited according to a screener about purchasing frequency. So, we ended up with two people in the session who bought the family buckets every week as they were supposed to, but, *"Actually eat it? Good God, no!"* Pretty embarrassing for everybody.

The thing is that it might not be obvious that we need to include a question about vegetarianism in a screener about fried chicken. However, if we are deliberately hiding the interest in chicken as opposed to other kinds of fast food, there is always the possibility that this issue will not get addressed because it doesn't come up. Therefore, it's really helpful if we can have a conversation with you about the kind of participants you definitely do not want in your session.

We would far rather get straight past any embarrassment or squeamishness about this, and make sure it's covered in recruitment. If your client is going to be viewing the groups and there is any possibility about negative sentiment towards their brand or even their category, let's screen out those people – we have had this with skincare brands, where we needed to avoid recruits with very strong opinions about animal rights or organic ingredients, because they might make helpful contributions, which affect what others will say also.

Another example – sun-protection products – was a

project during which one participant stated in her introduction that she had just recovered from skin cancer. That particular group's responses were not consistent with the other groups in the analysis, because everything everybody said was with the awareness of this woman's presence, and it impacted everyone's ability to be honest about how casual or inconsistent their use of sun-protection products actually was.

So spending a couple of minutes during the briefing considering what a particularly wrong or unhelpful participant might look like, in the context of a given project, can be time very well spent.

Incentives, Honoraria or 'Thank-You' Payments

Whatever we call it, you need to pay the people who are giving up their time to take part in your research.

Why do we pay incentives to market research participants?

"I don't want you to recruit me people who are just in it for the money!" – A refrain we've heard from plenty of researchers and we would agree wholeheartedly, providing that little word 'just' is given due consideration.

If you are a qualitative or user-experience researcher who cares about the work you do, we understand why you love it – exploring human behaviour and motivations is incredibly interesting and fulfilling. You take pride in doing it to high professional standards, you care about the people who take part in it (or you would not be reading this), and it brings complex personal and professional rewards of many kinds. However, we certainly hope you get paid for it as well.

Your time and your experience are worth money, the insights you bring add great value to your client's commercial enterprises and decision-making, and it is only fair that you should be suitably rewarded for that input. You wouldn't dream of describing yourself as 'just being in it for the money', but you live in a society where people get paid for adding value to other things. So your salary is your fair reward.

We believe the same goes for participants as well.

Rewarding somebody for their time and money does not mean that they are any less committed to the participation, indeed recognising it as of monetary value should mean that they commit more and make greater efforts. Very often, in consumer research, the cash incentive on offer compares favourably with the hourly rate they might earn anyway, and it is not wrong for that participation to be transactional in nature. You want them to bring thinking and effort to the process, not to passively sit there but to engage with your ideas, get their brains to sweat, and give you some great verbatims. We believe that appropriate payment for this, in cash terms, is a reasonable expectation.

There is a strangely British thing, that sometimes makes us awkward talking or thinking about money. Especially cash notes in brown envelopes. However, we all need to earn the stuff and spend it, that's how the world works, for most of us (we once recruited a fascinating project with more-or-less 'off the grid' lifestyle respondents, but I am pretty sure they got paid in cash at the end of it too, so there you go).

Interestingly enough, one of the few positive aspects of the financial crisis seems to have been a slight 'lightening up' and getting over this cultural hang-up, more willingness to talk openly about earning a few quid extra, and recognition of our individual worth as consumers. This is good for us in recruitment of course, and we hope that it is good for research overall – a greater appreciation of the value of the unique perspective every consumer holds. Whether it is people earning reward points for their supermarket shopping or sharing their email address in exchange for discount vouchers, people are engaging more with the idea that their attention has a price.

Even the way we use social media requires an acceptance and understanding of the fact that if we are not the paying client then we are the product – somebody is paying for our page views. So, it seems reasonable to talk more freely about earning some cash for sharing our opinions in research as well. People are more likely to share the opportunities we offer with their friends as well, which is great – a real win-win.

Paying incentives also recognises that people may have direct costs related to their attendance, particularly at a face-to-face event. They may have travel costs; they may be paying child-carers... They may simply have the opportunity cost of giving up their time: that's time that could be spent either earning a living, or doing something of their choosing – instead, they are spending it with you and your stimulus material.

So, the incentive on offer goes some way, we hope, to compensating and acknowledging that. Of course it shouldn't be the only reason that people participate, and we are very careful, in recruitment, to stress that they will all gain from participation, above and beyond the cash they take home. We also make it clear that they are being recruited to take part in an active process, not just to show up and sign in.

Getting contributions from every member in a group is part of your moderator skill-set on the night, and some people will always be more lively and forthcoming than others, but everybody we have interviewed will understand that the research is about their ideas and involvement, not about their presence.

With certain projects and certain kinds of participants, the need to earn cash isn't so much of a draw – in terms of what the payment means to them. Recruiting high net-worth participants, we may be offering them less than their professional charge-out rate, or pocket change to a well-heeled investor. However, we do have to offer the cash – even if we alternatively offer to make a charitable donation instead, on their behalf (and experience tells us that there will be very little uptake on this). Offering a fair incentive reflecting something meaningful to them, tells people that we appreciate what they are worth – not that we think they need the money.

A final point to bear in mind, is that whilst people gain many different things from taking part in research, they don't know about that beforehand. Nearly everybody we recruit has never taken part in anything like this before, and they're approaching it with a mixture of scepticism, curiosity, anticipation and possibly even slight nerves.

The feedback we receive daily from grateful participants suggests that they have an excellent and interesting time in every well-run research event we hold – they enjoy the social aspects of the research, they enjoy being listened to and having their opinions valued. They may also perceive great reward in their potential influence on a product they love (or hate). We have even had people specifically tell us they enjoyed it so much, they would gladly have done it without the payment!

However, those factors are intangible and individual, and, most importantly, they are reflections AFTER the event. We cannot persuade anybody to come along on that basis – what they each get out of it will be unique and intrinsic, depending on many different factors. We cannot motivate people to take part based on what intangible personal things they might gain. The cash therefore has a very important role in terms of motivating attendance in the first place, even if it is not the most significant factor finally, in what they take away from it afterwards.

Paying incentives - the nitty gritty

Paying research incentives ought not to be a complicated process, certainly not on face-to-face research events. They turn up, take part, and you give them an envelope full of cash in exchange for a signature on receipt. If you can get to a cashpoint and have access to a small pile of stationery, it really couldn't be more straightforward.

However, we do appreciate that for some clients, this might not be as simple as it sounds – access to cash might not be easy or practical, there might be policy or ethical issues that make this difficult.

We know, that particularly where group discussions are concerned, the actual amounts of cash involved can quickly get quite high, not something you would want on your personal expenses for the rest of the month or carried around in your pocket. That's why we offer a cash incentive handling service and will deliver envelopes via courier ready to disburse to your participants on a weekly basis. Most of our competitors and most research viewing facilities do the same.

We prefer to do it this way, rather than paying participants electronically, because this is what participants themselves have told us they prefer. There is something about cash-in-hand that maybe feels more rewarding and a bit more fun, as it does not get sucked into overdraft and bills and general expenses.

People might also need to pay cash out directly, for babysitters or travel expenses, so it's great for them to have it straight in their pocket. I feel it creates a very direct connection between the research they have contributed to and their reward, if they are paid by the researcher rather than by us, and right in the moment.

Of course, if there is a problem with handling cash securely at your destination, we can ensure that participants are paid electronically on the same day.

Owing to the vagaries of the banking system, they may receive the payment up to 3 days later, but we can at least let them know that it has been made and is on its way, or we can offer them a PayPal payment instead, which they can draw down into their current account very quickly.

Please note that if we are paying your incentives on this basis, we don't want to do so until you have confirmed to us that everybody we have booked has definitely turned up and participated satisfactorily. We will collect the payment details and preferred method of receipt in advance during recruitment, but we do not want to release the payment until you let us know you are happy. So, please give us a quick call as soon as the last ones are all seated.

What about vouchers? Well, these can be used in payment, but from our polling of participants we do have to reiterate that cash is almost always preferred – real money that you can spend anywhere – as opposed to specially restricted money, which has to be spent in a particular place.

Although there was one exception to that rule, in that Amazon vouchers seem almost as widely welcomed – which to some extent has replaced the universality of the High Street Retailer voucher... Do you remember when you received those for Christmas as a kid? There was a sense in which it could almost be better than real money that your parents might encourage you to save or do something sensible with, because it could be spent on a very wide range of things that were essentially luxuries and treats. Some people have told us they feel this way about receiving incentives in the Amazon voucher form, because they can't be spent on the gas bill or supermarket shopping but can be put towards purchasing things they want, rather than need.

They are also very quick and easy to administer, and 100% trackable. If you are paying them yourselves using Amazon vouchers, you can brand them by uploading an image and can make bulk payments rapidly... While keen to declare that we have no association with Amazon, their ubiquity makes them a straightforward option that is almost universally acceptable.

We would definitely not recommend the use of any kind of voucher to be sent by post, which is usable by anybody who receives it. Unless you are going to send the post by a tracked service, which costs the earth, the bottom line is that on any project involving 20 or more participants, where you do this, at least one will complain a week later, that they have not received it and the incentive will have to be replaced.

This is more a comment on the reliability of the postal service than the honesty of respondents, but when paying direct to a bank account, PayPal account or email address, we know and can prove that payment has been sent and claimed – which makes for a much more solid audit trail.

Given that vouchers are intrinsically slightly less valuable and flexible than actual money however, we'd recommend rounding up slightly, where possible, on the total payable.

When we are handling responses electronically on behalf of the researcher, we always aim to have the payments sent within 24 hours of that person's research participation. We want to make it as close as possible to the experience of getting paid cash in hand, in the traditional way. It might still be a couple of days before the payment clears into their account, because we dare not pay it in advance, so we feel a responsibility to initiate the payment promptly.

If you are paying participants directly by any means other than cash in hand, face-to-face, we will need to discuss with you exactly when the payment will take place, so that we can advise participants exactly what to expect. We do understand that you may not be able to make a same-day payment, particularly if you are in the midst of a massive fieldwork project. This need not be a problem provided we manage the participants' expectation appropriately from the start.

We do know from experience that any complaints about delays in payment will be made initially, back to ourselves, whatever we tell people about who is responsible for paying them – so we will request a named contact at your organisation to whom we can refer any queries with regard to incentive payments. The Market Research Society Code of Conduct is very clear that participants must not be misled about the terms of their participation, and an undue delay in paying a promised incentive would certainly count as a misdirection under the code, potentially one that could result in a complaint. Or, of course, you could simply get us to handle them for you…

A final point regarding the logistics of administering incentives… Please make sure you have enough of them, to cover any over-recruitment. If we are recruiting you 10 people for a show of 8 in a group, you need 10 envelopes, because if all 10 show punctually then they will need to be paid. If you can realistically only accommodate 8 within your group activity, then 2 get to go home straight away – often, believe it or not, genuinely disappointed at not being able to take part. At the very least, paid they must be.

How long after the start time it is reasonable to pay a latecomer is a judgement call for you to make, and we'd recommend taking into account the sincerity and calibre of excuse offered, whether they've called ahead, and whether they look like they've been hurrying. Around 20 minutes for a group discussion feels about fair, perhaps less so for an interview taking place in rigid back to back slots... Qualitative factors matter, always.

How much should you offer as an incentive payment?

When it comes to deciding how much incentive to offer, there are a number of factors to bear in mind.

One, is what everybody else pays.

Saros participants do not take part in repeated rounds of market research and, as soon as somebody has participated in an event, they are automatically suppressed for a minimum of six months before we start to invite them again. However, before they find their perfect match, they may well see repeated invitations for events for which they could apply.

They might even make repeated applications –many will have a good idea of the kind of incentive typically offered for a given kind of event, and there is a case for being careful not to go below the perceived 'going rate'.

Indeed we will be reluctant to take on any project that does not offer what we regard as a reasonable incentive, simply because we know it will impact both on the recruitment and on the turnout.

We are always happy to advise upon appropriate levels

of incentive for any job we quote on, and that advice will be affected by a lot of different things.

One is the typical expectation, of course, and there are also realistic minimum rates for face-to-face events.

It might seem strange that we would advise the same kind of incentive level for a typical two-hour consumer focus group as we would for a half-hour interview, but experience has shown that there is a definite 'getting out of bed' threshold below which it is simply not sensible to go, due to the associated levels of dropouts and no-shows.

We could only advise either speaking to them for a bit longer than you had planned to get better value from the incentive, or we will simply tell them it's likely to be 45 minutes or an hour – get them there a bit early to make sure your schedule runs like clockwork, and induce delight when they get done before they had expected.

Of course if the sessions are very short indeed, it'd make more sense, instead, to over-recruit by a larger amount.

Another thing that sometimes surprises potential participants is the difference in rate between consumer and business-to-business research. A participant told us that they were delighted to have been paid twice as much as they had received the year before, when they came along to talk about buying printer ink for their office – as opposed to the shower gel research they had taken part in previously.

Both sessions were the same duration, and they said they enjoyed them fairly equally. However, in the latter case they were being consulted about their professional opinion, of course, as a procurer of office consumables, as opposed to somebody who takes showers.

It is sometimes a little hard to explain to participants

why this is the case, but it simply is, and we do know that there are people who would never dream of applying for a £40 shower gel focus group... They sit and look out for the invitation that seeks their input due to their IT director status, and pays accordingly.

That is absolutely fine by us, we all wear many hats in life and perform activities of very different perceived value. Obviously we recruit a great many more consumer focus groups paying 40 quid and they have more opportunities to be an eligible member of one of these, so most are happy to apply for either.

If they wait for something more lucrative it could be a very long wait, as these opportunities naturally tend to be a great deal more specific and therefore harder to fit.

A further case where we would recommend paying a slightly higher than consumer incentive, relates to medical market research.

Anything where the level of disclosure and comfort is likely to be rather different. Asking people about their experience of a serious illness is a very different proposition from getting them to talk about washing their hair, it demands more emotionally, so it is appropriate to respect that by paying a bit more. This also recognises the fact that, for anybody with a chronic health condition, the simple act of participating creates more physical demands, particularly if travel to a venue is involved.

Sitting in a group discussion, maybe sipping a drink and joining in a general conversation, is obviously a relaxing and pleasant experience, considerably less intense, hopefully, than taking part in a depth interview or a user-experience session.

For this experience, in particular, we sometimes receive

feedback from participants, that they do find it stressful – not necessarily in a negative way, but it demands rather more concentration and effort from them than being part of a group. That's why we tend to advise a higher minimum rate is appropriate for anybody who is having attention focused on them directly in a one-to-one situation.

A slightly higher incentive in this event protects both you and us from the likelihood of a no-show as well, by providing that little extra motivation to turn up on time.

Part of the incentive payment is obviously intended to cover any direct costs they might have, associated with travel to attend, and as such you can pay slightly less for any remote methodology like online or telephone interviewing. Online, in particular, which might take place over several days, we can discuss and advise an appropriate incentive based on the total hours or minutes of intended input expected from the participant, to be paid as a single lump sum.

If it's a project of longer duration or takes part in several phases, it might be appropriate to pay the incentives in several stages. However, we would always recommend back-weighting the payment, to motivate completion.

For example, if your project consists of a set-up interview, followed by an online bulletin board, terminating in a big group workshop, we would suggest paying a modest amount of say a quarter of the total at the first interview – this will address any transport or other costs they have in attending, and show them you are serious about payment for the project as a whole. Then pay the balance once they have successfully completed all phases of the project, making them far more likely to go the distance.

When complex projects like this are in hand, we believe

it is best practice to advise participants exactly what each element is valued at, in terms of incentive payment. This helps them to understand the level of input and effort likely to be required in each case, for example we might say to them this project is in three phases and the incentive for each part is X, Y and Z respectively – the payment for Y and Z will be made together when you attend the final workshop.

In almost all cases we would recommend offering a single fixed amount for the incentive on any given project.

We will disclose that to potential participants along with the timing and location, and then it's up to them to decide whether it's worthwhile for them to apply, bearing in mind factors like travel time and cost.

This is far preferable to haggling over individual costs, and allows them to factor in their level of interest additionally, in applying for specific projects. We recruit for some games-testing clients that people will travel in from a huge radius to central London to participate in, and we know that if they are coming by public transport they could even be out of pocket – but the prospect of getting their hands on an unreleased version of their favourite title makes it attractive.

When it's a focus group about wallpaper adhesive, the relevant radius might be drawn a little tighter to the venue, but, if it happens to be near the office, then forty quid cash is forty quid they didn't have before...

Of course there are exceptions to the extra expenses rule when it comes to certain audiences, such as disabled people who may be unable to reach a venue by public transport, or require the services of a personal assistant or sign-language translator.

If a research activity requires participants to spend their

own money, for example in making a purchase from a retail outlet, then it should be made very clear what the basis of that purchase is – for example: *"The incentive payment of £60 is the rate for the discussion group combined with the pre-research store visit, where we expect you to spend between £5 and £10 purchasing an item of stationery from the specified fixture, and spending around 20 minutes writing about your shopping experience on the pre-research forum. You will need to bring the stationery item with you to the group discussion where we will photograph it, but you get to take it away home with you afterwards."*

If everything is explained transparently, there are no unexpected surprises or disappointments on the night and everyone knows what to expect. The incentives can they be handled very matter-of-factly and in the background to the research event.

Avoiding "Sugging" when paying incentives

The Market Research Society's Regulations for Administering Incentives and Free Prize Draws (https://goo.gl/CjelX0) is completely unambiguous on the definition of sugging, which means 'sales under the guise of market research'.

The relevant clause states:

> *Members must ensure that client goods or services, or vouchers to purchase client goods or services, are not used as incentives in a research project.*

The reason for this is that the research exercise must remain completely separate from any marketing or other kind of behaviour that is intended to influence the behaviour of participants in any way.

Research does not happen in a vacuum and being exposed to information about products/brands must inevitably make them think differently about them in the future, what we must not do is directly encourage them to try or buy the product. Offering the client's product, or a voucher to buy it, is a direct violation of the clause, because it is sure to influence their behaviour, relevant to the brand.

We appreciate that it might be difficult to say this to your client if they are generously offering a gift of a product that is attractive and valuable – however, we cannot use this to motivate people to attend.

In terms of the instruction above, we have to be extremely careful about making client merchandise available to participants at any time. In some projects however, and with certain specifications it might be acceptable to offer an additional surprise gift in addition to a stated incentive, after the research has taken place and only if the participants are existing customers. We would not mention this in recruitment.

It is, naturally, OK to distribute products for the express purpose of sampling or testing them as part of the research itself, and this may be in advance of the actual event – such as a cosmetic product which is to be tested over a few days at home as part of a pre-task, before attending a focus group to discuss the product with other testers.

It is NOT sugging if the product is issued for this reason, and generally such test products are supplied in non-commercial packaging anyway, specifically designed to obscure the brand – if the researchers want participants to respond to the product rather than their expectations.

Whether a test product gets fully used up in the testing

phase is something of a moot point, if it is not collected in afterwards, then participants are effectively receiving a gift of the rest of the jar... so long as this is definitely in addition to a fair incentive paid for all elements of the research activity.

Over-recruitment

You know how many people you want to talk to in your research – but, how many should we actually recruit...?

Why do we have to over-recruit, for qualitative research and user-testing?

Whenever we recruit participants for group sessions in qualitative market research, such as focus groups or creative workshops, it is standard practice to over-recruit.

However methodically and accurately respondent recruitment is conducted, the reason qualitative research exists as a discipline is that human beings and their behaviour are inherently hard to predict. People are changeable, flexible, occasionally perplexingly perverse and they are pressured by a wide range of different things, to which their responses are driven by multiple factors we aren't even aware of.

However important a research session is to the researcher or their client, or to us – trying our level best to recruit it, it is never going to be anything like as important to the participant.

That is the bottom line about which we can do nothing.

For participants, their stake in the whole thing is limited to that brief face-to-face session, and the fifty quid they are going to get for it. We try to encourage them to form some relationship of loyalty to us as Saros, but because we don't send the same people to multiple events they have less sense of letting us down and being overlooked another time, than they may have in other cases.

We therefore recruit as solidly as we can, focusing on booking in people who seem the most committed, engaged and intrigued by the whole event, the ones who assure us they are most definitely going to be there.

Our interviewers are extremely tenacious, engaging and persuasive, whilst at the same time qualifying anyone smelling remotely flaky, very hard.

We stalk them with reminder calls and texts to the point that they cannot possibly no-show due to lack of information or memory but could still change their mind and turn off their phone, should they wish, for whatever reason.

If something comes up at work, at home or socially that holds greater priority for them then, chances are, we will get a late cancellation, or worse still, a no-show ...and that's before we factor in circumstances beyond anyone's control, such as transport problems or a domestic emergency.

It is frustrating when occasionally we know that people are being fundamentally disingenuous about their reasons as well. I recall ringing a client at lunchtime on a Thursday, where the rain in London had finally stopped after many miserable weeks, and suddenly a warm summer evening beckoned. A quick decision to over-recruit just a couple more spares, meant that we did have a full turnout in the 6pm slot – despite half a dozen people suddenly finding themselves having to attend urgent meetings after work. It's enough to make one just a little bit cynical about human nature...

On another occasion where we had, against our best advice, been persuaded to recruit a job for a charity, offering a significantly lower than usual incentive – at which point, the reminder calls stage, it all began to dissolve suddenly with multiple withdrawals. Individually, every single one had a plausible-sounding excuse, but there was a very clear pattern of behaviour when the project was looked at as a whole.

Certainly, we must remember – the right to withdraw from any research project at any stage is enshrined in the Market Research Society Code of Conduct, and we mostly grit our teeth and stay professional when someone blows us out too late to make a replacement.

Of course, it is not enshrined anywhere that a respondent gets to let us or our clients down twice, and we keep very careful records of late cancellations and reasons given for them, so that our interviewers can make an appropriate judgement call should they prove to be a fit for anything else in future.

Hopefully however, the project is safely over-recruited, and it's more of a nuisance than anything else at this point.

If you are running a focus group of eight people it's fairly easy to recruit ten to the same spec, and then, if they all show up, discreetly pay off the final two when they arrive – or, perhaps, the two whose profiles make them least likely to contribute interestingly and effectively to the session. Your project manager can identify those for you easily and a sensitive and attentive viewing facility host can take care of the process on the night.

We are always happy to liaise directly with hosts on this. We value that relationship, knowing they can make or break your fieldwork on the night. Although a quick decision about who to pay off is likely to be random and arbitrary, as long as you get 8 seated on time, that's all that really matters.

Over-recruitment of groups is simply an insurance to make certain you have a full quota, with no room for doubt. Whether to recruit 9, 10 or even more people, to ensure your group of 8 seated, depends on a number of factors – including your incentive budget sensitivity, the target group involved and even things like the time of year or media events.

Depressingly predictable stereotypes inevitably come into play – unfortunately it is true that young adults, particularly young men, are most likely to no-show; busy professionals are most likely to cancel, and if there's something like the World Cup or big happenings in Eastenders or Big Brother at the same time, well, all of that has to go into the planning too. Remember – your priorities are not your participants' priorities.

Over-recruitment for individual sessions/interviews

Suppose you are running individual sessions, how can you and your recruiter work together to ensure you don't have any empty seats?

A single no-show for one-to-one interview is a hundred-per-cent empty session. Depending on the nature of the project and the fieldwork process, this could potentially be a disaster – so how can you plan to avoid this?

Firstly, as your recruiter, we need to know if some sessions are more significant than others, for logistical reasons.

Our interviews are those that speak to the respondents directly, and although endeavouring to ensure that every single appointment is booked in a rock-solid fashion, with reminders (within the limits of the local legislative frameworks on stalking), some people always come across as more reliable than others, as well as simply being more effective and engaged individuals. We'll make sure you get the very best of the respondents booked in for the critical slots, the ones being live-streamed to the CEO and her team in another continent or observed live by 12 people.

Of course, every session is important, and every session deserves the best recruitment – but humans are so qualitatively different that we can use this difference in the scheduling, to get the best results.

Incidentally, if one or two of the sessions are absolutely, utterly critical, then we can always over-recruit those. It's rarely practicable from a budget perspective to double-book 8 sessions, but the two that the board are going to be viewing live from the next room… let's get those double-booked, for relatively little extra cost in comparison to the opportunity cost of an empty seat. That's the thing we are all trying to avoid. Sometimes, of course, all the sessions are equally important and, unfortunately, we can never be sure where the weak link is – which one of the eight might no-show for whatever reason. As almost all the participants we recruit are first-timers there is rarely a track record to go on and, although our interviewers' instincts are finely honed, they are not infallible.

The best way to tackle this depends on your deadlines. If you absolutely MUST have those eight completed tests, and the timeline has a little bit of slack in it, let us schedule two extras for the following day or tagged on to the end of the session. Both can be cancelled and paid off remotely, the second you confirm to us that the final scheduled respondent is seated in the test room. Even if it results in your having to stay a bit later in the day, it's a good way of guaranteeing your full quota of tests by close of play.

Instead, if you could see them the following morning – even better – we will book them in then.

Of course, if not working in your own lab or you have a tighter deadline, this may not work, so a third option is to engage an extra respondent or two on a 'floater' basis.

This also works well when every test is viewed 'live', and you have to make every second count. Sometimes the best intentioned respondents wind up being late.

In this scenario, we'll simply recruit a spare who is offered a fixed incentive to be available and sat in the waiting room along with a good book, from just before the first session starts until the last scheduled person arrives. If anyone then no-shows or otherwise blows out on the day, they can swap in seamlessly to fill the gap. If you can keep them supplied with cups of tea and wifi access, then everyone wins. If you have a co-operative receptionist they may even be allowed to go for a walk between sessions, on the clear understanding that they are on the spot for every start time and don't wander too far.

This approach is obviously most successful when you have a consistent and straightforward quota – that is, all 6 test subjects are identically specified. If you have a split test going on where you are comparing results from 2 different operating systems for example, it may be best to cover all bases by recruiting and retaining a floater for each quota but, naturally, you don't want to end up with more participants being paid to loaf around the waiting room than are actually required in the sessions. Perhaps some of the segments are more vital to your research objectives than others, and these are the ones we can armour-plate in recruitment.

Obviously, it also depends on who the participants are. If your sessions are with senior business executives or medical consultants, it simply won't be viable to pay them to sit and read a book. A combination of different strategies and approaches will work on each project.

The main thing is to trust your recruiter with the backgrounds to your underlying research objectives and to the equally important objectives of best use of lab/studio time, incentive budget and achieving the satisfaction of internal stakeholders during the fieldwork sessions. We can make suggestions and try to come up with a plan that best delivers on the day.

Costs of over-recruitment

From our point of view, we'll always quote a group-rate that includes an agreed safety-net of over-recruitment. We'll bill that rate in full whether you get 8, 9 or 10 participants turn up, assuming the cost agreed was for a group of 8.

This actually protects us and we would always rather do it, it means we are not exposed when, hours before the group, one person is not responding to reminder messages. If we know we have 8 or 9 solid confirmed folks who are definitely going to be there, it takes the pressure off everybody – we believe recruitment should be done in a calm, attentive and professional way, not scrabbling madly around begging replacements a couple of hours before the group is due to start.

Simply put, if you let us recruit the spares earlier in a methodical and meticulous way rather than a mad dash-around in the final moments, they will probably be better participants. If they are not pre-tasked in any way, a last-minute replacement will simply be a less effective participant.

Costs of over-recruitment of individuals is different of course, as we will have to bill in full for every eligible participant who turns up, whether you can use them or not. That's why the section above outlines a range of the different ways we can approach this, depending on your budget and priorities.

The one cost that you are always exposed to in over-recruitment terms is the incentive – as regardless of whether you are on a group rate for us or not, if we're recruiting 10 people for your show of 8, you will need to have 10 incentive envelopes prepared for the night and if you are paying a floater to sit in reception for many hours, they will need to be compensated accordingly – we can advise on what is an appropriate amount, and what to offer depending on whether it's the 10:00am participant who no-shows or the 7:00pm.

A final point regarding over-recruitment, an obvious one which can nevertheless get overlooked …it can cost a lot more NOT to over-recruit, in the bigger scheme of things.

You might be renting a user testing-lab or a viewing facility by the hour; you might have disappointed stakeholders present; you might have a rigid deadline that allows for no mopping up another day …the real cost of all these can end up greater than the one for paying off one or two surplus participants.

If we tell you we need two weeks to recruit a particular target of participant, and you prefer not to budget for spares, then, on the day, someone cancels at 4pm in response to a reminder call, there may not be a lot we can do.

We might have other people who looked like good

matches in response to the online screener and, if that is the case we will try hard to contact one and persuade them to be available at 2 hours' notice ...but more often than not this is a fool's errand, because people have complicated lives.

We can't contact those spares in advance and tell them to keep themselves free in case of a last-minute chance to swap in, not without incentivising that commitment – in other words, effectively recruiting them as a spare.

Sometimes we can let a couple of people know that they are first in line for any cancellations, but we have to make it clear we do not expect them to hold themselves available.

Tangible and intangible costs of recruitment are complicated, and it's important to consider all factors that could impact on the success of your project.

Confirming and Instructing Participants

Once your participants are screened and booked into the session, the next stage is to confirm them in writing. Only after we have sent this to them, and they have confirmed acceptance, do we consider them completely booked into the project. At this stage then, having the written confirmation and joining details, a number of important things are going on that we need to get right, such as directions – getting you and your participants to the right place

First and foremost, this confirmation email serves to direct them to the exact location of the research. For any face-to-face project, we do not disclose the exact address until this point, because we want to ensure that only selected, confirmed and named individuals receive this information; so only the people you see on your respondent profiles will show up.

During recruitment we obviously indicate the general location and travelling distances involved, but the precise location is only revealed at this stage.

It is highly important for the punctuality and smooth running of your fieldwork that we are able to direct people completely and accurately. If there are any quirks about finding the location, for research, at your premises, this is the moment to let us know – about the roadworks blocking one of the main station exits, or the funny blue door they need to look out for.

We also need to be able to give them a contact phone number to use, if they cannot find the blue door – it is not much use anyone ringing us, as we have never been to your offices either. We will give them whatever information we can find to help them have a smooth and predictable journey, with a punctual conclusion.

We tell people to arrive on time; actually we suggest they arrive 10 to 15 minutes early – and we explain that this is to ensure that there is plenty of time to process the paperwork and make sure their incentive is paid. In fact, we'd definitely suggest paying the incentives at the end of your fieldwork session rather than at the beginning, if your hosting logistics will accommodate that – but you can sign people in and get everything started on time if people turn up in good time.

In our confirmation email we also stress very insistently the importance not just of punctuality, but of showing up in the first place – reminding them that they have been successful where others have not, how much they will get paid, and the importance of the event they are about to take part in. We remind them about any homework (see below) they have agreed to undertake, and anything they need to bring with them – such as proof of identity, or ownership of a qualifying product.

We include links to the Market Research Society Code of Conduct and other information about the event they are committed to participate in, as well as stressing their rights and how they will be protected throughout. We make it clear that cancellation at this stage is far from ideal, but if for any reason they cannot attend they need to let us know as early as possible, to give us the maximum chance to replace them for you.

If the research is taking place in a hotel or public building, premises you do not own, or a professional viewing facility, then it is also really helpful if we can tell participants exactly who to ask for on the night. If you are using premises with dedicated reception services, this would help to make everything run more smoothly.

If, instead, you are going to them, to interview them at home or work, then we will confirm the address back to them in writing, and politely request them to check it carefully straightaway. They need also to advise us about public transport and/or helpful directions or tips for finding your way to the agreed location. We'll include all these in the schedule we provide for you once recruitment is completed.

Pre-research tasks

Your project will very often require participants to undertake some kind of pre-task activity before they come. This might be in the form of a behaviour diary, a shopping exercise, or participation in an online conversation. This is part of our job: ensuring that all participants are fully briefed and prepared before attending the group, with their pre-task completed to an adequate standard, in good time to be of use to you in your analysis.

In order to do this, we need to understand the pre-task requirements in detail at the first stage of recruitment. We will always suggest that a suitable incentive allocation is identified as relating to the pre-task in particular: for example, we might inform participants, that the full incentive for the project is £70, this is £20 for completion of a pre-research task, which is expected to take up to one hour, and £50 for attending on the night with their pre-task completed. This avoids any doubt as to the importance of the pre-task, and also means it is completely acceptable not to pay the incentive in full if the pre-task is not completed.

We will always stress to participants that the pre-task is in no way optional, that being able to participate and receiving any incentive at all depends on turning up with their homework – no excuses, no notes from Mum, or saying the dog ate it.

We regard being able to advise participants as to the likely involvement and duration of the pre-task as an essential part of their informed consent. It is not fair to invite people to apply for a two-hour group discussion, then to inform them later that they will have to complete a written exercise first – we do know that this occasionally inevitably happens as discussion guides are developed and the brief defined, but we will always insist that an additional incentive is offered to reflect this additional requirement.

If they have considered that attending a group discussion for two hours is well worth £50 to them, telling them afterwards that they will have to spend another hour or so completing a written scrapbook first means that we are actually not being honest with them about the expectation – even if the incentive would have been adequate for the project as a whole had this been disclosed at the outset.

On the subject of incentives, one thing that we have found to work extremely well in the generation of high-quality pre-tasks, particularly those with a creative element, is to offer a prize as well as the incentives for completing it. If people know that they have a shot at an additional reward for producing something truly unique and special, some of them will really go above and beyond in their efforts. This works best if the pre-task is such that it can be reviewed and rewarded during the session itself, which if you are working alone may not be feasible, but for the kind of research where the pre-task forms part of the icebreaker or introduction then it might well be easy to spot who the standout contributor is and the prize is easy to allocate. Or you can instruct us afterwards whose day to make when we follow up, once you've had a chance to look at them properly.

We do completely understand that in many cases it will simply not be feasible even to glance at the brief tasks during the session itself.

We recognise that they will obviously form an important part of your analysis afterwards, but it simply isn't good use of the finite face-to-face time to look at the pre-tasks together.

We would ask you to consider the participants' reaction to this however, and make a point of acknowledging the receipt of the pre-task, and its role in the process as a whole. "*I spent hours on that, and she didn't even look at it!*" reflects feedback we have occasionally received, from participants who we have nagged and reminded to bring their pre-task with them but, on the night, they had been left with the feeling that it wasn't important to the researcher – because they were simply collected and put aside.

A brief explanation as to why the pre-tasks are important, and how they will be used in conjunction with the analysis from the discussion itself, is greatly reassuring to the participants who have worked hard to contribute their best. If this gets overlooked during a busy session, simply let us know and we can explain this to the participants when we sent out our follow-up thank-you emails.

It is easy to forget the fact that for the participants, the fieldwork IS the research project – they have very little understanding of what goes on, before or after it, to turn their comments during research into actionable insight for your clients.

Another important point about pre-tasks is that we must be able to give people a realistic indication of how long they will take to complete, and also whether they involve any deeply personal or intensive contribution. We have had people cancel late and withdraw from projects where it turned out that the pre-task – not sent to them until they were fully confirmed in the research – turned out to demand far more work than had originally been indicated.

Cancellations at this point where there is a big pre-task involved, throw a major spanner in the recruitment works …the last thing either of us want to happen.

The amount of time that people contribute to a pre-task will vary immensely, and depends upon a whole range of factors above and beyond the financial compensation. Many people love creative, scrapbook type tasks – we can screen for this during recruitment and make sure you get a team full of repressed Blue-Peter-presenter types if that is what you want, but we need to know about this up front, because other people might make perfect participants for a group discussion yet simply hate this kind of visual activity – if they cancel on receipt of the instructions, this again leaves us both stuck, with time running out.

There can also be issues to consider when the pre-task is more reflective or demanding emotionally than anticipated. We have had unexpected withdrawals when people received an exercise asking them to reflect on unhappy memories or difficult incidents in their past, or to reveal more than they are totally comfortable with about a personal situation. Once again, being forewarned allows us to be ready. There will always be someone else who is happy with that level of disclosure, who can be recruited instead, if we know in advance

As recruiters we are not able to provide help and guidance to participants in completing their pre-task – in fact we will request a contact on the research team who can answer any direct queries.

It does help to have advance sight of the document before deciding to whom we will send it.

It enables us to understand clearly what is expected of participants. It works better for everyone as we can then deal with queries without relaying them to you ...queries, for example, about whether collages can be created online and printed out, rather than gluing images onto a piece of paper.

If the task involves a diary exercise – looking at media consumption over a four-day period for example, is it acceptable for them to complete this on day four retrospectively? Probably not in most cases, I would guess, but this needs to be made explicit in recruitment; if committed to take part in this exercise they will need to find 10 minutes a day over the next four days in the run-up to the group to complete the diary rather than scribble something down on the way to the venue, based on unreliable memories.

Very few people aim to disappoint and submit an unworthy pre-task to a researcher they are going to meet face-to-face and spend a couple of hours with.

In the event that something is badly done or rushed, we can often trace the difficulty to ambiguity in the instructions, which could have been cleared up earlier in the process. People do have complicated and busy lives, they might be quite certain they can squeeze an hour into the week before the research to complete a pre-task, but if that pre-task turns out to involve something that can only be done in a particular time or location – such as visiting a fixture within particular store – that can scupper their best-laid plans. Again it all comes down to the fact that the earlier we, as your recruiters, know what will be required in the pre-task, the better we can select and prepare participants who will complete it usefully and well.

A final point about pre-tasks, that almost does not need to be made any more – except where there is a physical product to test or taste – it is much better if the pre-task can be distributed electronically rather than physically.

At the turn of the millennium when we started, it was common practice to send out large paper workbooks, single-use cameras, and all sorts of complicated packages to participants.

By and large the post office managed to deliver all of these successfully within a day or so, leaving little notes and tucking them behind neighbours' bins and so on, if the participant was not home… Sadly a lot has changed within the UK, and it can no longer be safely assumed that packages will be delivered and signed for on the day expected, or that neighbours will be pressed into service to accept delivery.

The last thing we want is for a week-long diary workbook sitting in a sorting office until the participant is free to go and collect it at the weekend.

If there is something to be physically distributed that will not fit through the average household letterbox, then we will need to make special arrangements to have it sent to them at work or to a trusted third party.

If we do have to deliver a test product, we would

suggest adding at least three working days to the timeline for the project as a whole, and also ensuring we have lots of notice to liaise with the participant about the best way to get the product delivered to them – especially if it's further complicated by requiring refrigerated storage, in the case of a food sampling project.

Nearly every logistical problem can be worked around with sufficient notice, but digitally redefining some old-school pre-task tools is a great solution for anything not involving physical product handling. Diaries, scrapbooks, workbooks …all are very easy to attach to a confirmation email, or there are purpose-built apps available, it costs nothing to do and requires no extra time. If we are sending an attachment with our joining details, we will always instruct the participant to make sure they can open and understand the documents included, before confirming they are definitely going to turn up and take part, bringing all of their pre-task requirements with them.

Changes to the Schedule or Brief

So, all the participants are now carefully screened, appropriately incentivised, confirmed in writing and well underway with their pre-task – however, we do know that, even at this stage, things can be subject to change. We also know that if you spring a change on us this close to the fieldwork, it probably isn't down to anything in the researcher's direct control either. Travel plans can become disrupted, stimuli may not be available, a test product may not get delivered in time – any number of things can derail our best-laid plans.

More frequently, change can come in earlier, when we are halfway through a recruit and suddenly the venue or sample has to change. The client has suddenly insisted on adding extra questions, which weren't in the online screener...

Perhaps we can ask them on the phone, but maybe the inclusion of these factors impacts on the incidence and even the viability of the recruit itself, or means we actually targeted a slightly incorrect group of people in the first place.

Such amendments are frustrating all round, but we will always try our best to accommodate them within the project plan. Once things are underway and a date is set, we will do everything we can to achieve it for you even if the terms of engagement significantly alter ...however there may be additional work involved.

Sometimes changes to the brief, once recruitment is underway, means that someone who we have already booked in is no longer eligible to take part, and we have to un-book them. This causes disappointment to the participant, who might have made many unsuccessful attempts to apply in the past and to whom we can of course make no promises as to when we might get a match again, but we will do our best to explain and help them to understand, as well as to manage any negative feelings developing.

If they have been confirmed in writing for several days, particularly if it is within 48 hours of the event itself, we will also suggest that the cancelled participant is paid some or all of their incentive payment – what is reasonable in any given incidence we can negotiate between ourselves at that point.

People do sometimes tell us they have booked time off work or pre-paid childcare in connection with attending – and we will ask for documentary proof of this, at other times we'll accept it as an expression of their disappointment at the moment.

It's surprising how people forget that any future offer to participate is within the gift of the interviewer they are expressing their anger towards, and not something they are entitled to in any way.

However, if we regard their commitment to attend as binding and firm from their point of view, if the event is cancelled, they have a right to feel let-down.

Also if they have been undertaking any kind of pre-task, they will need to be compensated for this, in a reasonable/proportionate fashion. It would be fine to ask them actually to submit the work they have done, in order to receive this.

Sometimes the research will be postponed rather than cancelled, but we always need to be very clear about the distinctions between these two states. If a project can no longer go ahead on the date set, but will instead take place in two weeks' time at the same time and place, we consider that's postponed – we will immediately book the participants into the new session, hopefully we won't have to replace any of them and it's essentially an administrative task.

If the project is definitely going to happen again, needs to happen for sure… BUT, we cannot be certain exactly when – then we have to treat it as a cancellation.

The project they were booked for is not now going ahead, and they may well be eligible for one we haven't got definite plans for yet.

So we can't ask them to commit to that, or to refrain from applying for other projects that might come their way in the interim.

You as the researcher know that whenever it is good to go, you're going to be part of it and make it happen – but potential participants cannot possibly relate to the event in the same way and will need to be properly stood down from this job, hopefully to be re-recruited when the time comes …if they are still available, interested and eligible at that point.

If for any reason a cancellation happens on the day itself, we will do everything we possibly can to get hold of and stand down every participant.

However, we would always ask that someone is on hand at the cancelled venue who is aware of the situation – people will have been sent joining details and advice for an event at this location but might have missed the message that they are no longer required.

We understand that the now-surplus participants for the project are just one part of the resourcing and logistical nightmare you will probably be tackling, in the face of a late hitch of this nature – so we will do all we can to help everything get managed smoothly.

Special Cases and Kinds of Research Participant Recruitment

Recruiting for Online Qualitative Research

One of the most positive changes we have observed over many years of recruiting for qualitative research, is the emergence of many excellent platforms for conducting research online.

While some methodologies have their limitations it can certainly be argued now that the tools available are genuinely qualitative, and their advantages greatly outweigh the disadvantages for many kinds of research and the recruitment that goes with it.

From our point of view working in database-driven recruitment, avoiding the requirement to attend a physical location to take part, is a tremendous boon to many potential participants. Because our advertising and PR is frequently targeted at a national level we have thousands of participants on our database who are never likely to be in a position to attend a traditional research event.

They might live miles from a viewing facility, have caring and domestic commitments, they might be disabled, or simply far too busy to make it to a group discussion – however – they would make fantastic participants for an online event.

When looking at a brief for online qualitative research, the first thing we will need to do is satisfy ourselves that the process is genuinely qualitative rather than quantitative – where different parameters apply (and we might not be the best people to recruit it). There are increasing numbers of projects that seem to cross-over, using a range of somewhat qualitative techniques but often working with very large numbers of participants, perhaps over quite a long duration and often with little interaction between the participants themselves. There is overlap here too with dedicated communities and panel type research.

Although happy to recruit for longer duration projects, we are not able to recruit panels for indefinite use by anybody else, because this would breach the agreement we have with our members.

Once we are clear that we are recruiting for a specific qualitative project, we will need to understand how your chosen platform works, in particular whether the research will take place synchronously or asynchronously. The technology is now widely available to conduct genuinely live online discussions that really do simulate a focus group, using anything from a freebie Google hangout, to bespoke videoconferencing software.

In recruitment terms this is directly equivalent to recruiting people to attend a focus group in a viewing facility: we simply need to ensure that in addition to other recruitment criteria being met, they are also sufficiently confident with the technology, and have access to minimum specifications of internet connection at the designated time slot.

We will need to understand about any device or browser requirements associated with your preferred platform too of course... Nowadays nearly everything works on everything, but we can never afford to assume that.

If the research is to be text-based but synchronous, then slightly different skills must be tested in recruitment. This is a much less common approach nowadays, but it does happen. The ability to take part in a rapid written discussion with multiple participants is not something that everybody will be comfortable with.

It has interesting parallels with the way we actually communicate within the team at Saros, being a dispersed remote working team ...all our meetings take place via a dedicated chat window, and when the discussion heats up it can be challenging for newcomers to follow.

People need to be able to touch-type in order to keep their place in the discussion and be able to read as other remarks scroll past.

Counterintuitively, it is actually quite important that participants in this kind of discussion are comfortable with the idea of typing a little bit inaccurately, and letting typos go by without being hung up on correcting them. We can test these skills directly in recruitment via an IM chat if required, and we will also screen for previous experience of this kind of environment, as well as their abilities with the keyboard.

It would be a mistake to assume that this kind of conversation is limited to certain age groups incidentally, there are plenty of mature and retired people who can out-type any Snapchatting teenager, with gusto.

Asynchronous research, which takes place via a written

discussion is more common, and infinitely adaptable to many kinds of participant. For this kind of recruitment, we will want to explore the familiarity with this kind of threaded conversation – are they used to taking part in forums or group chats of any kind?

Generally, even though we will telephone interview participants at some point during the selection process, in this kind of research we pay much more attention to their written responses, and we will use more open-ended questions during screening. This will require them to construct simple arguments and justify answers in writing. We'll use the word "why?" a lot more, to make sure that they can give meaningful written responses to qualitative probes.

A great many bespoke platforms now exist to facilitate this kind of online qualitative research, and make participation easily accessible across multiple platforms and devices, including mobile devices. Many also make it easy to upload different kinds of content, such as photos and videos and audio files – if this is going to be required in your project, we need to know about it so that we can screen for the capacity during recruitment, and also make sure that they have any minimum specification of device to use the app in question.

We might even test this during recruitment and ask them to submit a quick video or something else appropriate, if we have any doubt as to how best to select people who will make good participants for your project.

It is this kind of multi-platform asynchronous project that has caused the revolution in online research, and enabled us to bring together research participants who would never otherwise get to take part – and enabling researchers to work first-hand with inaccessible groups.

The feedback we get from participants is amazing as well.

We recruited a bulletin board of first-time mothers of newborns to research baby feeding activities, which turned into a highly supportive postnatal community, many of whom arranged to keep in touch online afterwards once the research itself was finished…

They had felt so connected to the other mums sharing their anxieties and frustrations and baby-moon love, and may still be in touch to this day for all I know. The researchers were delighted with the midnight breastfeeding video blogs, capturing the honest raw experiences 'in the moment' from this unique life-stage, involving participants who were rarely capable of making plans to leave the house never mind attend a research facility.

Which platform you choose is of course up to you, and they vary a great deal in price-point and capacity. We're always happy to discuss our experiences of those we have used and to feed back anything we've learned from participants too.

We will send out the on-boarding instructions to your participants in the same way as we would send out directions and addresses to physical locations, but it's important to stress that while we'll do everything we can to get them logged on and launched, we are not able to provide technical support for a third party platform.

This is very rarely an issue, because most of these tools are well-designed in order for non-technical users to get up and running fast – but it is worth mentioning because user-support needs and existing knowledge/experience vary so very widely.

Provided you and the platform provider have ruled out

issues with their login information, we'll probably find it easier simply to replace the participant, rather than struggle to include someone having insurmountable technical problems.

One very important aspect of recruiting and briefing participants for online research, is to make the expectations of levels of engagement absolutely clear.

If we are recruiting somebody to take part in a one-hour depth interview, their responsibility for that process is to turn up at the appointed time and place – after that, it's over to you, and of course we don't expect them to sit there with their mouths closed, but they know that their commitment is to be spend the hour doing research, and so long as they do whatever you ask of them during that hour then their part of the bargain has been kept.

Online research however is necessarily a lot more open-ended, and rather like the pre-task instructions discussed earlier, it's not fair to say participants haven't met expectations if those expectations were not made explicit at the outset.

For example, we'd suggest saying something as detailed as, "The bulletin board will run for 4 days, from the 17th to the 21st. Please check that you are able to follow the instructions to log on to the board no later than midday on the 17th, in order that we have time to arrange any help that might be needed. After that time, you can take part at any point to suit you and your schedule, but in order to earn your full incentive of £75 we expect you to log on and respond at least 3 times a day.

We hope the discussion will be lively and detailed, and we don't expect or require you to read every word of every thread, but for successful participation, each day we want you to respond to at least two of the questions prompted by the moderator, and comment or expand upon at least one of the remarks by your fellow participants, and we'd expect each response to be a minimum of two sentences long.

Of course we hope you will be motivated to get more involved in that and will engage deeply with the areas of the discussion that most interest you personally. As discussed there will be an additional £100 prize awarded at the end of the project, to the contributor the researchers feel has made the most effort to respond to others and really think about the issues being discussed."

Over the top? We don't think so, and being this granular in briefing means that nobody can say they didn't realise what was expected of them, or what the researchers needed from their engagement.

If required, we can easily supply a support moderator for longer or more extensive online projects, to help engage all participants.

If you are busy dealing with your stimulus and your clients' needs, it can be difficult to spot that participant 17 has actually not said a word since Tuesday, or suddenly went very quiet after that heated exchange on some irrelevant subtopic…

Having someone there simply to manage the participants, rather than the content of the discussion, can be one way of ensuring that there are no wallflowers or disengagers allowed.

We can also chase them up outside of the platform with a quick call if needed, to find out what is going on.

A final point to make about online qualitative research recruitment, is the question of cost.

Sometimes clients are attracted to online methodologies to save money, and this makes total sense. Travelling all over the country or farther afield to conduct interviews takes a lot of time and money, and there are many areas where savings can be made – on travel, logistics and facilities, even on respondent incentives when you are not requiring them to travel to a central location and they can participate from the comfort of home – but the one thing I would argue that you should NOT attempt to economise on, is the recruitment of the participants themselves.

Recruitment for online research is arguably MORE crucial than when you will meet your participants face to face.

In particular, we would not advise relegating recruitment to a company specialising in quantitative panels, and having no experience in qualitative recruitment.

Yes, I know, we would say that. But consider if you will, your own life online...

Chances are that, online, you present a range of somewhat varying personas. Depending on the circumstances and audience – your LinkedIn profile is likely to be rather different from your Facebook profile.

You may use a range of anonymous usernames to shop on eBay, chat on forums of interest, or to blog about your passions.

Not one of these personae is deliberately deceptive, although you may well feel some are closer to the 'real you' than others. The thing is, they each represent only a small part of the picture of what makes you who you are… You have constructed them, consciously or unconsciously, to present a particular face to that bit of the online world.

In real life we also create, construct and put on appearances as occasion demands but, face-to-face, it is much more likely that most of us are pretty consistent – it's easier to be ourselves and be a whole person, even if we do play multiple roles and wear lots of different hats.

Those roles – for example, parent, professional, artist, sports competitor – might in any combination be criteria for selection into a qualitative research event ...but the research itself would inevitably address and involve the whole person.

Your recruitment criteria would be contextualised and brought to life as a complete human, and a much rounder and more complete picture would be gained than could possibly be achieved when all you know is that they came off a panel as people who are interested in playing 5-a-side football.

When a trained qualitative recruiter interviews them properly, before you even meet them, you can be sure they didn't tick the wrong box on the panel, or sign up for every interest available to increase participation chances, or want to fit in just one more study this week in order to make a panel pay-out threshold.

If your research objectives are truly qualitative, it makes sense to invest in the selection and screening of your raw materials – the research participants – as carefully online as you would offline.

The possibilities offered by conducting increasingly qualitative insight studies online should not be compromised or cheapened by lowering standards in respondent recruitment and selection, as this will do the whole industry a disservice – and encourage the pigeon-holing of online research as a less effective and authentic option.

The alternative, is applying the same standards of participant selection you would apply to any face-to-face project such as a focus group or depth interview.

You then get the same standards of commitment, reminders and follow-up that you might expect for a face-to-face project as well...

We have heard of panel-driven recruits where no telephone interviewing is included, and over-recruitment of up to 300% is advised to ensure that enough people (whoever they are) ultimately log on to take part!

It's your project, you want the insights generated to be of as high a quality online as they are offline, surely?

Just our opinion...

Recruiting Participants for Usability and User Experience Research

Everything you have read so far of course, applies in full whether you are recruiting participants for traditional qualitative methodologies, or for a user experience interview/test. When we started out in the recruitment industry, user experience testing didn't really exist in the same way that it now does, and it was common for developers to contract with traditional qualitative suppliers in any case. Nowadays around 50% of the projects we manage our recruiting either for user experience laboratories, or for developers running their own tests in-house.

The approaches we use in recruitment are very similar, and not unlike scheduling a raft of in-depth interviews back-to-back at a venue but, for the participants involved, the experience can be very different, particularly if they have taken part in a group discussion before. Sitting with a group of other people chatting over sandwiches is a world away from sitting in front of a screen, possibly wearing eye tracking gear, almost certainly being watched directly through a webcam, and potentially feeling very highly scrutinised and exposed. The feedback we get from user experience test participants is usually very positive however and people truly enjoy the intensity of the process – although they do find it very full-on and demanding, certainly they earn their incentive, and consequently often feel that they have made a significant and meaningful contribution to how a product develops.

For our part, we always do our best to ensure that

participants know what to expect from their session, and if that means an intense one-to-one process then that is what they must be prepared for. We also explain clearly to participants that the word 'test' in this context applies to a device or application – it is not they who are being tested. This is very important, because even with the loveliest and most personable interviewer involved, participants can feel pressure when asked to perform tasks in a lab environment:

"Can you find the Contact-Us section?"

"Oh no! I can't find it anywhere! He's watching me and waiting for me to find it – I feel such an idiot... Now I am in a panic and it's taking even longer..."

...Helping participants to understand that, if an action is difficult to execute during testing, then that becomes a research finding, which is very important and of great use to the developers; it might mean that a button needs to be more prominent or simply that it isn't where people expect to find it. It doesn't mean they failed, or are rubbish at this kind of thing.

This is obviously relevant particularly to low-confidence users, and we make great efforts to demystify and explain why it is important for developers to access their opinions along with everybody else's. The more background we are able to provide, the better, within confidentiality constraints. We also use the most straightforward language and descriptions possible, otherwise someone might respond, *"But I don't know anything about navigation application testing! How could I take part in research about that?"* So it helps if we can explain from a very non-technical user viewpoint: 'Our client wants to know how people use maps and directions on their phone, so that they can make them easier for everyone to use in future. To do this they need to talk to people who hardly ever use these apps, as well as those who often do.' In other words, being able to explain to potential applicants that the research is about maps rather than apps, makes all the difference.

People are often quite bad at assessing their own levels of user-confidence when it comes to varying technologies. In screening we have various banks of questions we can use, to determine how we should classify somebody, particularly if a range of different levels are needed for testing. We have come across people who claim to be highly proficient and capable smartphone users, but who have never actually downloaded an app – they are just super-hot at using a couple of pre-installed games, and know for a fact they get higher scores than anyone they know…

Others use technology at work or home all day, and are quite confident with a specifically narrow range of tasks and tools that form part of their everyday world; in fact, they are the go-to person in their office for the jammy printer or how to use the shared address book, yet have no interest in what else technology could possibly do for them or the sheer potential of the equipment they use every day and actually type out as very low confidence users in many contexts.

We would suggest asking, in screening, about quite specific interactions with the kind of applications you intend testing, when it comes to judging proficiency and confidence. Someone might be a frequent user of social media and loads of other online tools, but would never dream of making payments or banking online, due to security concerns and lack of knowledge. They would definitely be a low confidence user when it comes to banking apps, never mind being in the market for peer-to-peer lending or investing online.

It makes more sense to get granular at this point, rather than relying on vague comparisons or how long they have been using certain things, and to zero-in quite specifically on the categories of interest. We can insert options such as to what extent they agree or disagree with things like, *"My friends come to me when they can't work out how to do something on their phone or computer,"* or, *"I really look forward to getting the latest updates and upgrades of any software and devices I use. Seeing what they can do for me is interesting and fun."*

One extremely important point when it comes to technical and IT competence amongst those '*in the know*' is a significant tendency to under-declare, which is not just about modesty. It's simply the 'Rumsfeld effect', conscious competence (or lack of it) – the more you know and the more unknowns you know about, the more you become aware of not knowing yet and the sheer scope of what is possible. So, being quite focussed on what is relevant to your project is what matters, because experts tend to be highly specialised in particular areas, and well aware of how narrow their field of expertise truly is.

Beyond behaviour and usage, we will also want to screen carefully for people who can interact effectively with whatever you put in front of them. This might simply mean familiarity with a specific operating system or device, or it might mean being able to use certain applications without modification or accessible technology.

Where we have had to disclose the device required or ask for referrals, for example if it's a very low penetration mobile handset we need to find, then we will always tell participants that they must bring the device with them as well as their contract or receipt, because the researchers will need to have sight of it to check it's definitely the right one.

People do get confused about their phones and also the software they are running, and it can be challenging to check this when we telephone interview people to book them, mainly because, at the time, they are probably using the phone in question to talk to us. But if a specific version of something like a mobile OS is required we can always direct them on how to take a screenshot of their 'about' details and send to us, by way of validation.

Usability testing can be very specific and precise, looking at users in particular and their journeys through a proposed application – checking for pain-points and observing behaviour, against precise clear expectations. We know that in some cases however you might be aiming to design something innovative, and need early feedback from potential users – without having anything coded or tangible to show them. The whole interview might end up being similar to some qualitative research exercises.

For recruits like this we focus strongly on imaginative questions, to find people who can project and associate – from the abstract to the specific and the other way round. Somebody who cannot look at a wireframe diagram and picture a full-blown application, won't be able to give you meaningful insight about their needs and potential uses of it. It isn't lack of intelligence in some cases or even a lack of imagination – it is just a particular way of looking at the world and organising their thoughts, but it makes them unsuitable for early-stage ideation and formative work of this kind. They would probably be the perfect participant for your last-minute sense-check prior to launch, where you want somebody to respond in a much more literal and immediate way.

When it comes to eye-tracking and use of webcams, people are generally a great deal more comfortable with these things than they were some years ago. Most people have web cams themselves on their laptops, they are used to video chatting for work and pleasure, and of course we live in an increasingly surveilled society generally. Again, we would suggest explaining it in the session, just as we would to prepare people in recruitment – and it's helpful for people to understand how the footage will be processed and used. Explaining that their eye movements will be used in aggregate with much larger numbers to produce a heat map, is both interesting for them to know, and simultaneously takes off the pressure and any self-consciousness about their eye movements, which are simply not significant on their own.

When any kind of headset is going to be worn, such as for mobile eye tracking, again we would prefer to be able to let participants know in advance about this, and if there are prerequisites due to the equipment then of course we must be told – for example, we might need to screen out wearers of certain kinds of spectacles. We even had problems once with somebody wearing very heavy mascara – I think she had false eyelashes – that stopped one of the eye tracking beams working effectively!

We know that most modern equipment will not have any of these problems, but set-up in different labs varies immensely. So the more you can share with us about the types of activity that will take place then the better job we can do – not only of preparing participants for what to expect they settle down quickly, but also finding the right participants in the first place

Finding committed and punctual participants is obviously very important for UX tests where lab time might be expensive, and with individual sessions the best way to over-recruit (see above) will have to be considered carefully. Ensuring that the schedule actually works for all parties, with sufficient breaks and set-up time incorporated between the sessions as necessary, will also be very important.

Unlike typical qualitative research, we understand that a great deal of UX testing needs to go on during the working day, due simply to the availability of facilities. Of course this does affect recruitment, because not everybody can commit to attend hour-long sessions during business hours, despite the fact that the incentive on offer is generally a little bit higher than for group discussion work. If it is really important that the views of working people are represented within your testing, then offering one slot as late as possible – say 6 PM – means that we are able to address this.

Also, if you as the researcher don't mind eating your lunch at a slightly odd time, then having slots at midday and 1.15 means that some people might be able to extend a lunch break slightly to take part. Given the intensity and individual nature of testing, it probably isn't an ideal activity to take part in at the end of a long day in the office in any case.

Obviously, if you are working with test products and applications, we appreciate that there is slightly more that could go wrong, than for the average qualitative researcher presenting prepared stimulus boards to their group discussion. Things might or might not be ready for testing on the scheduled date, and expectations may not be met, particularly if the user does something that wasn't planned for.

In this case it is likely that the research participant will be left with an uncomfortable feeling that somehow they were responsible, particularly if the session has to finish early – so we would always urge you to consider their feelings in this event and reassure with sincerity. We have had people call us in distress, thinking they have done something terrible to your equipment...

We know that sometimes when it comes to testing technology there will be last-minute changes and cancellations too. Unfortunately, while understanding the reasons behind this and that it is a risk at all times, participants have no stake in your management of uncertainty or what you are trying to develop. If they arrange to come and take part, are booked and confirmed, then the session is cancelled at short notice, we would expect them to be compensated.

There are many developers for whom we do regular recruitment who actually keep a range of standard tests up their sleeve that they can run if something goes wrong in the immediate build-up to testing. Rather than cancel they use the fallback tests to gain comparative data or confirm what they already know, given that the participants and the lab are booked anyway.

So whilst recruiting participants for user testing is not that different from recruiting qualitative depth interviews, we do need to consider a range of different needs on the side of the participant as well as the researcher to ensure everything runs smoothly on the day.

Recruiting for sensitive subjects

Recruitment of qualitative research participants for most fast-moving consumer goods or other markets is a relatively straightforward matter. As part of the screening process a range of open and closed questions is asked, to determine a match with the profile the researcher needs to consult with, in order to address their client's research objectives. Apart from screening out due to using the wrong combination of brands or other behaviours that are not required, the risk to the applicant is minimised.

A well-designed initial screener will ask the right questions quickly, and a few minutes of a potential participant's life is a reasonable exchange for the possibility of being invited subsequently to a well-paid focus group or depth interview on that subject; that is what our entire business is, after all, predicated on. It seems to work OK.

It's very different however when the subject matter of the research is something awkward or sensitive, because there are cases in which simply answering the screening questions – for which in many projects the majority will screen out and get nothing anyway – could become potentially detrimental to the respondents. When that is the case, things need to be handled a little differently.

Consider in the UK the old fashioned approach to focus group recruitment using face-to-face intercept methods – no problem stopping people in the street with your clipboard to ask them about their preferred brand of detergent, but how could you feasibly move the conversation on, to determine whether they were or were not in the market for incontinence products, or a weight loss magazine?

If the questions would have complexities and nuances which would affect their delivery in face-to-face recruitment, then those same factors need to be carefully borne in mind for online screening. Even in database-driven recruitment where initial contact is made by email, much more care must be employed when inviting members to apply for projects that are highly sensitive.

Often of course, decisions about who to long-list and invite to apply are driven by simple demographic factors; proximity to the venue is one, but other known factors exist, such as age. We simply don't hold detailed information on our database about most of the things we'll need to query to recruit them for any given project. That is what makes the screening process so critical, but being selected to receive a personally-addressed invitation makes people feel that they have been matched with it in some way at least, and this in itself is value-laden:

...“What on **earth** was it, about my profiling information, that made you think I might be interested in a project about (debt counselling / illegal downloading / sexually transmitted diseases)?!” is not an unreasonable response when you think about it.

So we will always do our best to take great care when crafting an invite, explaining that the qualifying factors for the current project are highly sensitive and we really have no idea who amongst those listed may qualify as we don't hold this kind of information – but we really hope you won't mind taking a look in case it is of interest. Often, it might be appropriate to reassurances about the relevant codes of conduct protecting their confidentiality and privacy within the research process itself. Borrowing from gamification approaches, spelling out the terms of engagement helps to embed the acceptability of the idea for potential participants, and enables reassuring mention of any other factors that might raise the comfort levels – such as the use of a female moderator, so it's all ladies together in a group about 'women's problems'.

The standard screening techniques of obscuring the 'right' answer amongst a raft of dummy ones might also be inappropriate here. Respondents are not stupid, and if the one sensitive or awkward response is embedded in an anodyne list it will stick out like a sore thumb anyway. Very few people are likely to attempt to feign embarrassing diseases or circumstances in order to try to qualify for a focus group.

In some cases it would be better to ask directly about the key criteria, then qualify on the screening interview – with respectful and relevant probing. This will establish the qualification directly and appropriately using robust validation techniques where appropriate after the fact (such as asking people to send us a quick snap of their medication's packaging so we can confirm this with the project sponsor), *"Because we're not doctors, we're market researchers."*

Whilst for most research projects we would tend to avoid public social media postings that can be viewed by anyone, in favour of individual invites to pre-screened people, there is definitely a valuable role here when it comes to sensitive topics. Bulletin boards or forums of communities of interest might be an appropriate place for a shout-out so that people can choose to respond or not, without feeling singled out individually. Providing a clear call to action and an easy, no-pressure response mechanism can help here. People are often surprisingly happy to recommend or refer others when they can do so in a safe and regulated way.

The problem with screen-outs is also one that must be handled very delicately, when the subject matter is delicate to start with. You can tell people that to qualify for a research project they are using the wrong mobile phone network – but you can't tell them they have the wrong kind of cancer, at least not in the same way.

As a rule, we never tell people why they haven't been selected for a project, because – not to put too fine a point on it, it's generally none of their business. The deal-breaking question is usually one that would reveal far too much about the background of the project itself anyway.

We also avoid entering into any kind of dialogue with people about the possible reason for their being rejected, nor do we want them trying again from an incognito window with changed responses… (no, most wouldn't but occasionally the lengths to which people go are frankly astonishing). As a rule, we simply won't reveal what it was about the combination of answers they gave, which on this occasion made them an unsuitable match for the project in hand.

Unfortunately, this sometimes leads people to jump to their own conclusions about why they have been rejected and, if there were sensitive questions in the screener, they are the ones people tend to remember and will be the ones by which they feel most likely to have been judged. We know it is far more likely that they were eliminated because of their mobile phone network, but what they occasionally fixate on, when they screen out, are the facts that we asked about their religion or their sexuality.

It doesn't matter how carefully and neutrally we explain, it's merely that disclosing specific types of information are intrinsically higher-stake risks than others.

We need to recognise this when writing screeners, even if only to include reassuring statements about how we want to ensure the participant selection includes all sections of the community (often the case with publicly-funded studies, and something people are used to seeing in this context). However, we will not be untruthful if such a sensitive factor is asked as part of screening, rather than for monitoring.

If asked to apply selection criteria such as race or ethnicity, we will only take this on where there is a definite research-based reason for it that we can disclose to participants if challenged. This is part of our own non-discrimination policy.

An example of a project in this category would be when recruiting research for branding a cosmetic range targeted at black skin-tones – there would be no point whatsoever recruiting white women who would never use the range. Where possible we'd still rather go on self-selected behavioural questions, e.g. *"Which of the following ranges of make-up do you use...?"*. That might not always be a viable approach if you want to talk to women who don't use make-up currently, or it's a brand new product. In that case there is a perfectly good reason why the recruitment process will need to discriminate along racial lines.

It's a situation we have to monitor carefully in recruitment, because part of the reason we pioneered database-driven recruitment in the UK was to widen access to participation. This is good for research, and good for the community as a whole; people who were not personally known to an old-style recruiter were never invited to take part in anything. But removing barriers has a cost. and it's easy to be structurally racist (or some other kind of 'ist') due to laziness or lack of awareness.

Take the situation where we are researching a haircare product, aimed at typical European hair-types. It's fine to say we are going to screen out people with afro hair types during recruitment, because they are not the target for this product, and use completely different ranges of products for their haircare and styling. However, it is not OK to say we will only recruit white people, or English people, to be on the safe side and avoid having to make this distinction – that is indirect discrimination.

Similarly, when it comes to language and accents.

If research is to be conducted in English, then it's a completely reasonable requirement that every participant is highly competent in both expressing and understanding English; that's not discriminatory, it's simply essential. Furthermore, somebody might have excellent understanding and be really articulate in English, but might have a strong or unusual accent, which makes them completely unsuitable for any group discussion – it doesn't matter, we'll screen them out of the group but tag them for future one-to-one work.

Even so, it is definitely unacceptable for our interviewer to avoid calling people with foreign-sounding names, for fear that they turn out to have strong accents.

Nationality and residency also have valid reason to be screening factors in many cases. If someone is conducting research in the UK and other markets, it's reasonable to expect that their UK groups will comprise the normal ethnic and cultural variety expected in the diverse communities that live there, but they should be made up of people who actually DO live there – not transient workers.

If markets are being analysed comparatively, it would distort and confuse things to recruit expats in any of them. For other projects, length of residence might be paramount: where people grew up shaped their attitudes and values. Global marketing and branding strategies now converge increasingly but this simply wasn't the case when most of us were in our most formative years. The way household brands were advertised to us might be completely unique to the country we grew up in, and diverse products and names associated differently in dissimilar markets.

That seems pretty obvious to those of us working in research, we're used to recruiting groups observing reactions to rebranding and acquisitions …but it must sometimes be explained to potential participants, because it can feel like an unfair reason to screen out.

Basically, we just need to be a bit more aware of participants' overall feelings if asking potentially sensitive questions in screening. Questioning people about their sexual preferences is different from asking about their shopping preferences. We won't make a big deal of it but we must recognise their right to regard it as a bigger deal to answer some questions than others. When people essentially make themselves vulnerable in screening by revealing private and potentially embarrassing information, then they need and deserve extra reassurance about how that information will or will not be used in future.

The MRS, and every responsible code of conduct for our industry, require that respondents are not disadvantaged in any way due to their involvement in market research, and while we can never mitigate any disappointment at failing to be selected for a particular study, it is not reasonable that anyone is left wishing they hadn't applied in the first place.

Needles in haystacks: recruiting low incidence participants

There could be many factors that combine to make any particular recruitment exercise more difficult than another, however when qualifying recruits are extremely low in incidence to start with, that's clearly one of the biggest challenges.

Often that is exactly the reason you have come to us to find these people, you know that they are thin on the ground, and whatever their stake in the research outcome, we will not find many of them to screen.

There is often nothing that can be done from a design point of view, because this specific rarity is precisely what makes them necessary to you in the first place. The purpose of the exercise is perhaps to bring together people who would never normally share and collaborate on ideas, because of their uniqueness, the act of simply convening them can be highly synergistic... All we have to do is find them. Faced with one of these recruits there are a number of possibilities we could explore that can hopefully shift the challenge from impossible to merely difficult.

Firstly, if your single deal-breaking recruitment criteria is, in fact, that most highly elusive and low incidence one, we will look at whether there is anything else restricting the search unnecessarily. That would typically be parallel assumptions about where the crucial people may be found.

For example, we might be seeking users of a particular personal fragrance product. The manufacturer's data and history suggests that this product is typically purchased and used by women in their 40s, from a particular socio-economics background. Being aware of this can certainly help us target our recruitment efforts where we expect them to be most fruitful – however, restricting the recruit to AB women aged 40 to 50 would be a direct hindrance.

Although in any small sample the impact of demographic outliers must be borne in mind, it is always possible that the purchasing data is out of date anyway and surely the most important thing here is the current immediate behaviour.

It could be that the expectation is based on research conducted a decade ago, and a particular cohort of loyal purchasers, now well into their 50s are still buying it regularly. Or the product could have got noticed by a new group altogether… This could be due to a random endorsement or unexpected social phenomenon that has caused a new wave of slightly younger fashionistas to start experimenting with it. Either way, if we restrict our invitations within rigid age parameters, we will not locate these people – nor will you unearth the findings behind the shifts it indicates.

As we want an accurate reflection of current activity, with every recruit we would always suggest adopting a blind-recruitment approach based on their current behaviour and attitudes:

'Which of the following brands of fragrance have you purchased for yourself within the past six months?'

'How frequently do you use the following fragrances?'

'Which of the following value statements do you feel most strongly apply to the fragrance brands listed?'

If there is any doubt at all as to whether or not somebody is actually a consumer of the desired item, then an approach to validating this must be found.

Unless the item is incredibly rare and our recruit is likely to depend entirely on referrals, then it should not be possible anyway for applicants to second-guess the one we are interested in. But one easy way to validate the ownership of a bottle of perfume would be to ask potential participants to submit a photograph of their favourite fragrance bottles arranged on their dressing table. In this example, it would also be a great way to contextualise the purchase – does the brand we are interested in reflect their typical tastes and expenditure, or is it a rare aspirational treat, based on the other items they use regularly?

It might even make sense to split two apparently equal groups along these lines.

If we find this approach of opening up the recruit is starting to yield progress, we will keep throwing numbers at it – but our database is finite, and different demographic segments in different areas contain different numbers of potential participants.

If we have a few places yet to fill, and are aware that recently we have often researched in this segment, we may have to ask you to waive the six-month exclusion rule.

If we know that a great many of our well-heeled Birmingham ladies in their 40s have recently taken part in other projects, we might request your permission to invite them to help fill the remaining spaces – providing that other research has been about other subjects, and unlikely to influence their thinking about fine fragrances or their behaviour in your group.
However, suppose the incidence is really, really low in the first place, due to dispersion of the qualifying factors?

For example, a rare medical condition? There are a number of strategies we can discuss between ourselves, to enable successful recruitment for this type of project.

One potentially controversial approach would be to abandon blind-recruitment altogether, being specific about exactly what interests us, and asking directly for referrals. This only works where there is potential to validate externally the eligibility criteria, and on the understanding that there is no commercial reason why we must not disclose the source of interest.

We contend that it is only fair to ask people to refer their friends and family providing there is a good chance of there being a successful match... We cannot ask people to refer their friends and family for mobile phone research, but might be able to ask them to refer people who have a specific, unusual, or newly-released handset.

To ensure a robust recruit we would always validate, so we could ask people to refer anybody who they know to be suffering from a particular illness and, as part of the screening for the recruit, we can ask about their prescriptions and medications, as well as symptoms, which would only be known to a genuine sufferer.

It is hard to imagine somebody going to the lengths of googling symptoms and prescriptions for rare medical conditions in order to bluff their way into a market research project, but whenever there are cash incentives on the table we do consider the possibility, and take specific steps to ensure the recruit is robust despite the eligibility criteria having been unblinded. We could also ask them to bring their medication and prescription along with them to the research itself.

This can also work well with luxury brands and big-ticket items, such as cars or designer gear. Most people who spend large amounts of money on luxury goods are very clear about their reasons for doing so, and often happy to take part in a pre-task stage involving submission of photos of themselves enjoying their purchases and discussing what personal meaning they hold. If the occasional person drops out due to inability to produce proof of ownership of the sports car brought along with them on the night, then it's a great way for us to tag a potential time-wasting fantasist for the future and replace them in good time; one day we will publish another book, called, "Brilliant excuses from failed respondents", including the gentleman who had the misfortune to put ALL his car documents through the washing machine on the very day that the vehicle itself was stolen and destroyed by joyriders… That publication might take a while, because we have heard everything you could possibly imagine.

Unblinding the requirement in this way is also a great way to get people to recommend their friends. They might not have the right kind of car, but if there is one in the car park at work they probably know who it belongs to.

Obviously this becomes a trickier recruit because it takes a time to network this.

People need time to recommend their friends and get the word out, and it only works in categories where it is likely that people know about their friends' eligibility. Rare illnesses not so much, but exotic holiday destinations, designer handbags, or anything else people brag about socially, can all be great for this.

For some recruits we'll go one further and run specific advertising on social media, designed to funnel the correct people through to us directly.

If we are still struggling to find anybody eligible after exhausting our database resources and potential referrals, of course we will talk to you. It may be there is something we could address in the methodology itself, such as moving the fieldwork to a different location, if we have reason to suspect that incidence might be higher there.

Is there any alternative to convening a face-to-face group discussion?

If the recruitment could be done in-home, would that make it more viable, particularly for unwell participants or those spread over a wide area.

Would depth interviews, either face-to-face or on the phone, be an option?

If depth interviews are simply too resource-intensive, could some or all of it be done online instead?

In terms of successful database recruitment, asynchronous online methods are the ultimate level playing field, because it enables us truly to recruit from our biggest possible pool of potential applicants – including those who are miles from any kind of viewing facility.

If we are struggling with a very low incidence recruit, the one thing we will always try to do is offer suggestions as to how things might be unstuck.

We want to avoid ever saying, "This cannot be done," – because somehow, nearly always, there is a way it can.

It just requires a new way of looking at things. Occasionally, it might mean our outsourcing some or all of the work to a specialist recruiter, who has particular networks and connections in a niche area – we certainly do not mind doing this with our network of high-integrity suppliers.

This would take slightly longer, because we have to validate each recruit ourselves anyway and only tend to do this where there are specific and specialisms on offer, because we know that our database and resources are already extensive.

If it is a general consumer recruit that cannot be

fulfilled via our database, we are confident enough to say to you that we believe it is incapable of being fulfilled.

Only when there is a specific advantage will we recommend a third party, such as a medical recruiter who has a network of consultants who can refer their patients for research.

Another thing we will always endeavour to do is be completely transparent about what the problems are, and what to expect.

If a recruit proves simply impossible, we will try to identify this as early as possible in the process and work with you to make changes, making it doable after all. If alterations are impossible, we may have to state that there is nothing further we can do.

For example, if we have spent 50% of our possible invitation resource in the London area and generated not a single successful recruit, we will have sunk considerable expense into getting the job to this point.

If we had taken on the work, it would have been done at our own risk, so it is unlikely that this would happen – hopefully we are sufficiently experienced to discern the difference between a good professional challenge and the utterly impossible.

What we will not do is invest the remaining 50%, throwing good money after bad, unless there are corresponding shifts in the methodology or eligibility criteria to direct things towards a viable recruit. Nor will we tell you that things are likely to change in time when they are not – just because we have another five days in the timeline.

If we know there is nothing we can do to progress the work we will tell you, rather than wait for a miracle.

It is important to stress that identifying the difference

between a tough low-incidence recruit and an impossible recruit is something we are pretty good at. Hopefully we will have this worked out before work even starts, only accepting the task on the basis of whatever conditions are required to make it doable.

Low incidence recruits are interesting and fun, and they challenge our ingenuity to come up with successful ways of reaching out to the right people.

We are quite prepared to depart from our database where required, to go where these people can be found – there is a secret corner of the internet for every one of us. Perhaps we can advertise there, finding a way to present the research participation opportunity as intriguingly and attractively as possible to catch their attention.

If participants exist, then we will find them one way or another. It might cost a little more and/or take a little longer, but we learn something from every difficult job we take on that helps us with the next one.

Recruiting people who definitely don't need the money

Certainly, the incentive payment is, or should be, far from the main reward for taking part in market research, even if it provides an important initial motivation.

The people we recruit report all sorts of benefits after the event in the feedback they share with us, but they share it because they are surprised at how they feel, the extra benefits – such as feeling 'listened to'. Feeling able to make a difference, in connection to a brand they know, is unexpectedly pleasant and rewarding. I am sure these are not their reasons for signing up to do it in the first place, so offering money matters… At least it matters to most of us.

So then how do you recruit high-net-worth people for whom no incentive payment is going to make a difference one way or another: people who really genuinely do not need the money?

The challenge here becomes one of marketing as much as matching. Presenting an intriguing and interesting proposition, and going further than we usually would to present the intrinsic rewards. People who spend large amounts on brands and services expect high standards in return, and they often do have a genuine interest in providing feedback to those brands in an appropriate way.

This is true even of time-poor senior professionals, and then it may become a question of balancing the challenges of the diary against their high expectations from the companies they spend their money with and the opportunity to have direct word with them. Sometimes being a good customer is just not enough, and the chance to affect how your frequent flyer programme or investment portfolio management company develops can provide a reward in itself, when presented in the right way. Everyone has some interest in making the world around them better, and people who spend serious money – on travel, gifts, fashion, transport or gadgets – are demanding and discerning consumers with expectations of excellence.

While money might not be the same motivator at this level, other human factors apply more. Curiosity and brand relationship really matter. If you have a passion for a particular fashion designer or sports car manufacturer, the possibility of seeing and even influencing the development of next year's model can be a powerful encouragement. With this kind of recruit incidentally pointing out in recruitment that they will be required to sign a confidentiality agreement really helps build the intrigue, and we've often suggested it might be required when it hasn't yet been discussed with the client. Helping consumers to connect with the brands they love and shape their future is a privilege that money can't always buy.

Naturally when it comes to encouraging participation some research topics will always be more attractive than others. Luxury brands associated with their personal values, which they actually like and want to help, are much easier to recruit for than any that sound boring or unpleasant.

One of the most difficult categories we recruit in involves participants of high-net-worth to talk about financial products – it is simply not the case that all people who have large amounts of disposable income are personally interested in talking about how they might invest it, and there are often very real concerns about confidentiality. Whilst we can tackle the latter head on with reassurances about the Code of Conduct and their protections, we cannot make a proposed discussion about pensions or insurance sound particularly sexy or exotic.

Appealing to self-interest with hopefully the right amount of persuasiveness is our best shot, but there are elements of the screener design that are particularly important when it comes to high-net-worth participant recruitment. Keeping things short and sweet particularly online seems to make a big difference to completion rates. Levels of overall scepticism and indifference are likely to be higher amongst those for whom the chance to earn 50 or a hundred quid is really neither here nor there

Unfortunately, although consumers at this level are rarely motivated to participate in research for financial reasons, that doesn't mean you can avoid offering a generous incentive payment to reflect the significance of the interaction.

We can always offer to arrange a donation to a charity of their preference as an alternative – simultaneously acknowledge the value of their input whilst recognising they don't actually need the money.

Without wishing to sound cynical, it is a genuine reflection of our experience that unless some current disaster appeal is happening, very few participants will opt for this.

The key is in making the research participation attractive for its own sake, finding a reason beyond the financial transaction to engage drivers such as curiosity, self-interest and feelings of exclusivity, amongst such far-from-typical research participants.

Recruiting participants who know each other

People usually choose database recruitment as opposed to traditional methods because they want to be absolutely certain that the participants in their group discussion will *not* be known to one another. When recruitment is conducted in a completely independent way rather than through networking, it means that the group convening is actually a genuine group of eight strangers – rather than a couple of pairs of friends, some people who have referred another person, and a pre-existing mishmash of relationships and group dynamics.

However, the research methodology sometimes dictates that participants known to one another are actually required. Examples of this would be a paired depth interview, which might explore how friends or family members use a product together, or a friendship pair in order to hold one another accountable and avoid aspirational or socially desirable responses in an emotionally loaded category. At other times it might be a larger group, a family taking part in an ethnographic encounter, or a group of friends who are going to talk in a group to a researcher about a shared activity or hobby.

This has a few implications in recruitment, and it has to be borne in mind that it represents in many ways an unusual divergence from our natural database-driven approach.

It might sound counterintuitive, but it is almost always going to be quicker and cheaper for us to recruit 12 individual interviews, rather than six friendship pairs. Why is that the case? Well, it's because we can recruit the 12 separate interviews independently, and effectively, simultaneously. We will invite all the people we want to screen online, and from there, our best matches to call, until the 12 slots are filled.

However, in the latter scenario, we first have to recruit the six people who are going to be our lead respondents. As well as ensuring they are a perfect match in terms of eligibility for recruitment, we next have to explore with them, thoroughly, the need for them to recruit or nominate potential connected participants. Then we have to screen our way through their list of possible partners. This inevitably takes longer, because they have to talk to their friends, seeking permission to pass their contact details on to our interviewer. The call then has to take place, and so on.

Further complications potentially arise, depending on what makes the partner/friend eligible in the first place. Sometimes simply being 'the person I lift-share to work with' might be sufficient to make them eligible. Then the main second stage of recruitment simply consists of making sure that the partner is definitely available for the session date, and putting them both down. This is a diary exercise and takes slightly longer than a single screening interview naturally, but is generally relatively straightforward.

However, we will always ensure that the partner does have a live conversation with our interviewer, simply in order that they can have any questions or concerns addressed privately, also enabling our interviewers to satisfy themselves that the referred person is committed and able to engage well with the subject to be discussed.

At other times the friend will have to fulfil complex screening criteria in their own right. Some of the screening factors might be known to the lead respondent – for example if we say we would like you to pair up with a friend around the same age – but at other times it will involve complex behavioural or attitudinal factors, which take much more detailed screening.

Difficulties arise when we are applying complex criteria in recruitment generally, but normally have our entire membership database to work with. Depending upon how absolutely weird and wonderful your criteria, we know that we have thousands of members we can potentially push through the screening until we find you the perfect match. However, our lead respondent's personal address book 'database' is likely to be somewhat smaller than ours and we can potentially place them in embarrassing situations if, after screening our way through several of their friends, we have to say that none of those were any good – *"Do you know anybody else?"* This can even lead to the primary respondent getting fed up with the process at this point, and after repeated calls withdrawing from the recruitment themselves... By which point the deadline for having completed recruitment is likely to be getting very close.

So you see, whilst on the face of it finding six respondents and then recruiting a further one each through every one of them sounds easier, when they all have to be screened properly, it is in fact definitely not. Sometimes there can be over-reliance on people to know people similar to themselves. If we are required to apply rigorous social behaviour criteria to the lead respondent but it's then left up to them to bring along four friends who share their certain preferences, this can have surprising results.

Occasionally, in this scenario we have had researchers complain… *"But the friends were nothing like them at all!"*

This really doesn't sound too surprising when you think about it, because my own friends are a highly diverse bunch – I would not want to socialise with people who were exactly like me, that would probably make for a pretty boring evening. Just because people share one attribute – perhaps a bunch of mums who are all in a WhatsApp group together for a pre-school – that tells you very little about what they are actually like individually and how they use the app more broadly. One of them turns out to be a messaging aficionado, whereas another only installed it and uses it because of this mums group... This finding might be valuable, but it will not make for a homogeneous group discussion.

If the timeline, budget, or preferred methodology does not allow us to screen the referred respondents properly, we can make no guarantees about what they will be like, and have to put total faith in the lead respondent.

They are obviously highly motivated to ensure that the

group comes together, but they are not research recruiters.

Of course, if your interest as the researcher is purely about how they use that shared WhatsApp group, then the group discussion will be fine – because that is the unique factor they all have in common. The difficulties only arise if surmising from it that they share other attributes, whereas in fact this does not get tested properly in recruitment.

Naturally with many audiences, it is the shared activity that matters, and there are lots of examples where pair or small group methods work extremely well. With children and young people, it can be a huge reassurance to be able to pair-up with a buddy instead of talking to a stranger alone. and some subjects that are frequently researched are those that simply don't take place solo – shopping, socialising, and playing certain kinds of games.

A further important point about friendship groups like this, this is one time when it is certainly totally appropriate for the research to take place in the lead respondent's home. They would need to be paid an enhanced incentive anyway for tapping their address book to support the project, so for this to include a hosting fee as well, in exchange for their hospitality is perfectly reasonable. Effectively this encompasses a fee in addition for referring their friends and family as secondary participants

The main thing that we as recruiters will need to be clear about when taking on projects of this nature, is the degree to which the referred respondents will need to be screened, and precisely how the recruitment timeline is therefore going to work. With proper planning from the outset, anything is possible.

It is worth saying that of all the positive participant feedback we receive, taking part in research along with one's friends has got to be the thing people LOVE most of all, and talk about in the most glowing terms afterwards. Being paid to have fun with your mates – what's not to like?

Recruiting participants from lists

In a way you could say we are always list recruiters. We recruit from our own list of folks pretty much at all times, rather than going out to find people for each job as it comes up …but when we talk about list recruitment, what we generally mean is recruiting from somebody else's list rather than our own. This distinction is very important.

When it comes to a member of the Saros database, we not only know quite a lot about the person referred to, we know about the data as well. We know exactly how recently updated the record was, where it came from, why they were registered in the first place (including being able to track in many cases which advert or piece of content prompted them to register), we also know that they have given us explicit permission – even encouragement – to contact them about paid market research opportunities.

When it comes to costing and planning for a list recruit however we have to take somebody else's best guess as to all of the above, sometimes the researchers' best guess when they have no real idea other than that their client has told them they *"have a list"*. So the quality and provenance of lists we are offered varies immensely – it's always somewhat of a step into the unknown.

This is assuming that we can use the list in the first place, because that depends on what permission the people on it have given to the data controller, the owner/processor of the data. Specifically, if it's consumer rather than business contact data, we need to know that they have given two kinds of permission – one, for their contact information to be used for the purposes of market research, and secondly that they have given permission for their information to be passed to a third party for any purpose (that would be ourselves).

Basically, we cannot contact them unless we know that these criteria are satisfied, and we are often surprised when asked to do so. Working with people's personal data as we do gives us great respect for how it is used stored and shared, and we have had people send us unencrypted lists they have no permission to share with us in the first place, sometimes containing far more information than we need. Unfortunately, even a very well-managed list might be impossible for us to use, if the people on it have never given permission for that use in the first place.

Hopefully the data has been collected with future market research uses in mind and explicitly opted-in though so we get past the first possible hurdle. Then we need to look at the quality of the list itself...

For one thing, the way a list is segmented matters a great deal, in relation to screening for the project. Sometimes the fact that somebody is actually on a list given to us at all might mean they are highly likely to be eligible, because they are known to be a loyal product user of 18-24 months duration in the midlands area, or whatever – the data is managed and segmented for the client's own use, and they simply require a certain number of people from it screened for suitability and booked in to the project (of course we always check for those eligibility factors at the point of recruitment just in case, but it very rapidly becomes apparent how good a list is in these terms – or not).

Such a list is also likely to be highly up to date, containing phone numbers that are current and live, reaching names that correspond to the data we are supplied with, and still check out on the eligibility factors.

At other times, when the data is current and up-to-date – we don't get a whole load of discontinued lines or, heaven forbid, discontinued persons (yes that happens) …but data might be completely unsegmented with regards to qualifying criteria. We might, for example, be given a list of mobile phone numbers from all over the UK, to recruit to focus groups in a specific location. All we end up doing in this case is causing disappointment and frustration, and this can end up having a direct impact on the reputation of the brand we are representing – which we have to disclose, if asked where we got the number from.

It is surprising how often this happens, and it generally means that a list has been extracted from a client database without the little extra thought that would have extracted a much shorter and tighter list in the first place. If the strike rate is low this can make cold-calling very unproductive. Another factor is the relationship with the brand we are working for – calling a list of passionately loyal customers is always considerably more effective than calling one of lapsed users, and occasionally we find ourselves talking to a very dissatisfied customer who has lots of feedback to offer the company concerned – and doesn't want to hear that our interviewer is not best placed to take that back to the relevant department at this very moment.

Cold-calling is not the only way to work a list in recruitment; often, it can be the very worst way. Our approach to doing research recruitment has always been to put the participant in control of the timing of the interaction. We send them an email with a link to a questionnaire and they respond to it in their own time, only if they are interested and available for that project.

Even though they have given us permission to contact them whenever we want about research projects, we almost never call them without checking out these factors by email first, because calling somebody is intrusive and disruptive.

This appears to be a trend in wider society, for both business and interpersonal communications, for better or for worse, we don't call each other.

We can't know what we are interrupting on the other end, and even if we are expecting an immediate response it is far more common these days to send a written message of some kind.

Many people can hardly remember the last time their home landline actually rang – never mind the last time it rang and it wasn't cold-caller, or somebody with bad news.

A lot of people will not answer unknown numbers anyway, on any phone.

Therefore we prefer to take an opt-in approach at all times with recruitment, and connect with people by email first. That's fine when it is people on our database from whom we have explicit permission to make contact in this way, but when it comes to client data, the email needs to come from the list owner/registered information controller.

Our preferred model for approaching this is to set up a brief opt-in form, perhaps with a little light screening such as availability and session timings – and have the list owner send this to their members.

We can provide brief copy explaining everything they need to know, which means that the only people who do apply are already interested and available, as they have passed their contact details directly to us for use in connection with that project.

We avoid all complications about transferring data from one organisation to another, and put the participant in complete control of the process.

When our interviewer phones they obviously have to go through qualifying demographic data in more depth than they would for one of our registered members, but at least they are doing so knowing that this contact is welcome and expected and explicitly opted-in to.

This is particularly important in some markets which are more sensitive or confidential than others. We have tried to cold-call lists on behalf of financial services providers, for example – and even with the hottest, loyalist, best-managed list in the world, the scepticism level is set to stun. Having to explain that we are calling on behalf of a brand-name they love, but we aren't from the company ourselves, and we want someone to come and talk to them about their savings or insurance products, is often a complete non-starter. *"...and you say you're going to pay me money if I let your colleague come to my house? Do I sound like I am one-day-old!"*

We have even had complaints from relatives of older people we have called on similar projects, accusing us of goodness knows what kind of frauds and scams – frankly it's a disaster. Far, far better, if the list can be not only warmed up but opted-in in the way described above. We can even give them the option of telling us when they would prefer or prefer not to receive the call, so that we can be certain to avoid family mealtimes or anything good on Holby with a badly-timed interruption.

When it comes to business-to-business recruits, this is still the preferred approach. The expectation and permissions around contacting people by email for business rather than personal addresses are slightly different – but we all know there is only one word for business email that is unsolicited and unwelcome, and if you're lucky the only response you will get is a quick delete.

We still will not send emails to a list supplied to us by a client, because we don't know anything about the deliverability or its authenticity. That list could contain spam-traps or trigger junk tagging, which could impact on the deliverability of our next email broadcast to our registered members. We don't recruit participants or clients by sending unsolicited email, as a simple matter of policy. It is definitely preferable if the client themselves can make contact in the first place, and introduce us as their chosen supplier to recruit a research exercise aimed at making their customer's experience better.

And in any situation where we are contacting people on behalf of a brand, using contact information which is not 'our own', we will always need a named individual client organisation to vouch for our bona fides and for the research exercise in question.

In fact, we would always encourage anybody with any concerns at all to contact the commissioning organisation for reassurance if they wish – we would much rather have them do that, satisfy themselves that this is genuine research exercise completely OK to take part in, rather than have them no-show on the night because of their unaddressed concerns.

So whilst recruiting from a list sounds straightforward and easy, there are many different things to be aware of, and the best way to handle that list might vary from one project to another. In some cases we will ask for permission to free-find as a back-up, if we are seriously concerned about the provenance of the data but the recruitment criteria itself make the recruit viable without it.

Recruiting children and young people

If you really want to know how good your product or idea is, perhaps you should ask a child.

Whilst children have their own behavioural codes and inhibitions, they are less likely to pull punches about the emperor's new clothes. They will tell you what they really think.

Of course in many cases children or young people are the intended audience/customer for the product being researched anyway, and in this case it is absolutely essential to consult them.

Whilst children are less likely to be the actual purchasers in most cases, their relationship to the gatekeeper to this purchase is absolutely fundamental, with more and more brands and services arising specifically to market directly to impressionable young minds.

Pester power has a greater role every year, and as children become empowered and enabled on and off-line, their role as consumers in their own right also cannot be overlooked

Luckily for researchers, children generally really enjoy taking part in qualitative research, user-testing and sharing their views, being listened to – indeed many of their motivations are exactly the same as for their parents.

Working with children as research participants is obviously a different proposition from working with adult participants, but the insights gained can sometimes be even more valuable and interesting.

We have been recruiting young research participants for many years and, although we ask more questions of the researcher initially when young people are involved, there is always going to be a recruitment strategy we can agree on that will help you to achieve your research objectives and consult the opinions of young children.

The safety and well-being of research participants is always our primary concern, working within the Market Research Society's Code of Conduct – but when it comes to young people, welfare and ethics naturally take an even higher priority.

For a range of good reasons, we do not store details of children as members on the Saros research database. For one thing, children cannot give informed consent to register as market research participants. Every time we recruit young people to take part – and in this context anybody under 16 is a child participant – we do so through the parent/guardian. Their consent and involvement is required at all times, and it is their listed dependents on our database whom we are searching and approaching in this way.

The invitation and screening request will always be sent to the person in this parenting role, and we will want to give them as much information as we can about precisely what the research involves. Ideally this will include more detail than is typical because, normally, we cannot say much about the discussion guide and its contents ahead of the research itself – in order to ensure that participants are not influenced. Parents of younger children though need to know exactly what the research will be discussing, and what activities and exercises would involve their children

We also believe they also have a right to know and understand the underlying intention behind the research.

When applying to take part in paid commercial research events people usually have an understanding that the ideas they share will be used to sell things to people.

Confidentiality and commercial sensitivities mean that this is often all they need to know, but parents of young children expect appropriate and indeed necessary explanation in more detail as to why children are being targeted for this research.

The reason might be utterly commercial, for example to make sure that a new edition of a computer game provides exactly the right degree of challenge to users in this age group – but parents still deserve to know this and if there is any 'greater good' benefit – such as benchmarking gaming behaviours of neuro-typical children, in order to facilitate adaptations for children with different needs – then parents also appreciate hearing about it.

Understanding the kinds of exercises to be used will also be helpful for parents in deciding whether their child will be interested and have fun with the research on offer.

With grown-ups, this is less of an issue – they are receiving their £50 to show up and do what the researcher requests them to do for the next two hours, and if they also enjoy it that's a bonus. As research activities vary so widely, and parents know their children better than anybody else, we find it makes for better as well as more ethical recruitment, to be able to explain in greater depth.

We might explain, for example, that the research will require children to look at images of products and discuss what they are reminded of; researchers will then ask them to draw pictures representing the different snacks they prefer to have in their school lunch.

They will talk in groups about why they chose those colours to represent them.

Obviously, this would be far too much detail to share with the actual participants in advance, but the parents are not the participants in this case – they just have to assess whether or not the research would be fun and appropriate for their child. The super-fussy eater or art-hater might not be a good bet here.

Parents are also the best placed to judge how their child will respond socially, because children vary so much in their interpersonal and communication skills, so it's very difficult to make assumptions simply on age.

Simple shyness, and how they are with strangers, is an incredibly individual thing - and also varies between boys and girls.

We have learned in recruitment not to be afraid to probe a bit on this, and to take into account social desirability and pride/competitive parenting, to work out who will really be OK chatting in a small group or even individually to a researcher (however lovely and personable the researcher is, as well as hopefully very experienced at working with young participants).

It would rarely be appropriate for us actually to telephone interview the young participant, but we're not afraid to ask detailed questions about how they like to interact; it is in nobody's interest for a tongue-tied, shy child to be forced into a session by a pushy parent for their own reasons.

We're looking for parents who are very clear about the reasons why their child would enjoy taking part, based on their personality and their interest in the subject itself.

Understandably when children are recruited as research participants, the telephone conversation usually contains just as many questions from the parents of potential participants, as are asked of them.

Even though the feedback we receive from parents of children who have taken part is overwhelmingly very positive, they naturally need 100% reassurance about the activities, ethics, safety, and expectations.

In particular parents will want to know who will be talking to their children – is the interviewer specially trained and experienced working with children?

Will the research be video or audio-recorded in any way, and if so what are the precise uses of the footage?

Is the interviewer male or female and do they hold a current valid CRB check?

We would not say that this final point is an essential one, and this is not the place for a detailed discussion of the extent to which CRB checks do or do not keep children safe... However, the fact that a research organisation has voluntarily complied with this is a reassuring signal for parents that child protection is taken seriously. It also shows that they evidently work with children regularly enough for this to have been a worthwhile exercise.

Certainly from a recruitment point of view, if the police check is held, we will reference it in the invitation to help reassure parents and encourage them to apply – so it is certainly a plus point that will facilitate obtaining the best participants for your project. We would recommend that anyone doing face-to-face work with child participants, whether in their homes or at your premises, should apply for this check and keep it up to date.

Depending on the age of the children involved, parents will also be keen to understand their own role in the proceedings. If the research involves attending face-to-face at a venue, the parents will need to chaperone to the premises at the very least, and it may well be more appropriate for them to be in an adjoining room, or even in the same room if the children are very young.

They might be taking no part in the research itself, but it is reassuring for a child to be able to keep their parent or guardian in line of sight if they are tiny. From a child-protection point of view of course this is also optimal, that the children and parents are never actually separated.

With slightly older children they might not need this degree of reassurance in order to be effective research participants, but the parents themselves might appreciate being able to view the research directly via mirror or video link. For teenagers and adolescents this might be neither appropriate nor necessary, but for any participant under 16 we will suggest that a parent is needed to accompany them to the venue and to sign for their incentive and willingness to participate, and that chaperone will require a waiting room/space, perhaps some refreshment as well.

In many cases, and if this will not be disruptive to the research, it would be helpful if they are able to bring with them other children – such as siblings of the research participant – who are also in their care, particularly if the research takes place after school.

We do know not every viewing facility waiting room is built with this kind of occupant in mind, so we'd rather check that out well in advance.

We will liaise with you in terms of briefing the parent/chaperone about what to expect, and also what is expected of them. Occasionally there can be issues with their understanding of the need to let younger children speak up for themselves... While the presence of Mum might be helpful in lowering inhibitions, they may need to be asked politely not to jump in if the child is hesitant, or if they disagree with what their child is saying or want to expand on it in their own words, and so on.

If we are recruiting a child-and-parent paired interview for you, that's different, but assuming it's actually the child you want to hear from, we will do our best to manage the parent's understanding of their role in this process, and suggest they bring along something good to read to pass the time.

The chaperone will also need to be paid an incentive – less so for their time than if they were an active participant themselves, but they are still taking time out of their day, and may well be incurring travel and other costs in order to attend.

When it comes to incentivising child participants themselves, this is one of the rare occasions where we'd suggest that a non-cash gift might in some circumstances be more appropriate, especially if they're very young.

If Mum gets 20 quid in cash to cover the travel costs, it helps to distinguish the two elements of the payment clearly by offering the child something completely different, which cannot be used to settle any grown-up boring bills, and is therefore totally distinct as being for the child themselves to enjoy and feel rewarded.

Whilst being careful not to contravene MRS guidelines on 'sugging' by offering gifts of the clients' own merchandise, something like a toy or a book might be a nice and widely-acceptable gift.

Remember that most under 16s cannot easily shop online in their own right, so if vouchers are used then it should be something they can spend without ID or accounts being needed, and choose from a wide range of things that might interest them.

Whilst the UK high street seems to have far less choice about it than it did in decades past, something like a W H Smith's voucher remains broadly acceptable, and means they can choose from a wide range of fun stuff for all ages (whilst parents and researchers alike can convince themselves that they are probably investing in a book or something useful for school).

Speaking of school, the scheduling of research with young participants can throw up a range of challenges, depending on the age groups involved.

During term-time, it can be very difficult to arrange centrally located research with young children, whose day often finishes late and involves complicated arrangements with child-carers, after school clubs, and the needs of older and younger siblings. Not to mention homework …to the extent that we sometimes have to manage unrealistic researcher expectations of slotting in multiple groups or depths back to back, in the crowded window between school end time and everyone getting to bed.

School holidays are far more flexible, although it's well worth bearing in mind that these are no longer universal fixed points in the calendar. Even adjacent local authorities can fix completely different weeks for half-term breaks, and also start and finish the longer holidays at very different times. All this information is usually publicly available well in advance though, so it just takes a bit of planning and accounting for, to get the fieldwork schedule right.

One thing to consider is weekend fieldwork – yes, it's a lot to ask of the interviewer at the end of a long week's work, but for getting groups of children together in central locations, it's well worth bearing in mind as an option.

Another is go to out to where the children are. This could be literally where they live. In-home interviews may be both easier to arrange, especially after school, and also reassuringly familiar for very young children, as well as potentially assisting the qualitative process with a bit of contextualising the participant from an ethnographic point of view. Young children may prefer to show than to tell, and being able to point to things or demonstrate how they play with them for example, might yield much greater insight than sitting them in a viewing facility.

In-home though, you are more likely to have their responses influenced or possibly inhibited by the presence of parents, siblings, pets, background noises etc. which may or may not have a negative impact on achieving your research objectives.

Many researchers prefer individual or small group work with children, rather than the typical full focus group numbers. Even if closely matched by age and gender, it can take longer for children to warm up within a group and start communicating with the researcher effectively, never mind with each other.

Teenagers in particular are likely to be far more self-conscious about how they come across to their fellow participants than to the adults paying for their opinions, more keen on establishing their position within the group, and this can be detrimental to the study in hand.

Without wishing to resort to tired old stereotypes, unfortunately teenage boys effectively can be struck dumb in mixed-sex groups, so most researchers find they get more from participants by splitting up boys and girls once they are old enough to notice the difference – a phenomenon persisting well into young adulthood for some participants.

A compromise between in-home and central interviewing might be to recruit in a more suburban location than usual. This is something that in general recruitment terms we try to avoid, because the feedback we get regularly from our clients is that they prefer the fact that participants recruited our way are more diverse and representative of a larger area...

Recruiting for an event in Central London for example, you get people who live all over inner and outer London, as well those who commute from much farther afield.

If you recruit an event in somewhere like Ealing or Bromley, you will by and large tend to be recruiting people who live in Ealing or Bromley respectively, because they are unlikely to be commuting in an out from distant areas, and quite often public transport between one suburban region and another is very limited, compared to going in and out of the city centre.

Traffic and parking too can be an issue, especially in the after-school rush.

Also, there is a greater chance that participants will turn out to be known to one another from a purely coincidental point of view... Almost impossible when you are recruiting from the whole potential population of London or Birmingham and assuming most will have some degree of travel time to the venue, but far more likely when you are recruiting families with kids in a narrow age band all living in the same school's catchment area. So, this might or might not be an approach worth considering.

Which bring us on to a brief reflection on methodologies with kids, and why this might not be such a bad thing anyway.

In fact, recruiting in pairs, or even small groups of friends, can be a good way to break the ice and enhance disclosure and norming in a group of children faced with an unfamiliar researcher and subject, helping them to feel more comfortable getting started and saying what they think.

In some cases, a friend can provide accountability and grounding – *"No you don't, you're rubbish at that game!"*

In other areas, where the subject matter is private, embarrassing, or subject to social desirability or aspirational factors (particularly amongst insecure teenagers) this might be the last thing you need. With adults too, there are some subject areas where the controlled dynamics of a group-setting can serve as a release – teenage personal problems that they never talk to their friends or parents about, but if they find themselves in a group of strangers who they will never see again, sharing this one common factor – such as an embarrassing health condition, or academic challenge – they could potentially open up in ways that would be difficult to achieve in a one-to-one conversation.

With younger participants the issues are very different and finding shared activities is the fastest way to break the ice. Gamification techniques are an essential part of every qualitative researcher's toolkit, and making the research exercises fun and creative is a great way to both norm and settle a group to get everyone engaged. Even gently competitive activities can work well, providing that the participants feel completely secure about the terms and what's expected of them, and that the requirements are 'fair' for all – young children have a profound sense of right and wrong that can be triggered unhelpfully if anything too adversarial is set up in a situation already unfamiliar and challenging. It is far better to make sure everyone is a winner, and that activities are collaborative and build on each other's contributions, to make something new and exciting.

Props and toys are always good fun and might be more important than with mature participants who are better at projecting and visualising. Children have fantastic imaginations, but different frames of reference from grownups – far better, for example, to show a big colourful poster of what a game or app might look like, than a detailed wireframe indicating functionality.

A model or prop is better still. In our experience every researcher will be genuinely surprised by some of the ideas and insights coming from the youngest of participants but triggering those ideas in the first place is best done without relying on intangibles and lengthy explanations – far better is finding a way to demonstrate instead.

Older children and teenagers have their own issues about how they communicate, which can make for challenges in research settings. We once had feedback from a researcher about a group of 13-15-year-old girls who 'wouldn't even look him in the eye!' It turned out that despite this initially off-putting introduction the girls had apparently come up with some brilliant stuff in the session, they just didn't cope with group interaction in the same way as a different generation.

If the researcher had been a parent of teenagers he might not have been as surprised, because they even collaborated with each other well in the group and built on one-another's ideas after some initial shyness. Their generation simply communicates differently ...and sometimes make me wonder whether we will still be recruiting for traditional group discussions in a few years' time.

He might have had a more overt response by letting them all text their introductions to each other or something.

Finally they communicated with both him and each other in a way that worked and synergised effectively.

Remember that, overall, the feedback we get from parents about kids taking part in research of all kinds is that they really enjoy it and, by and large, for the same reasons as grown-ups; someone is taking the time to talk to them about what they think, and genuinely interested in what they have to say. They get to see or play with new stuff, like a forthcoming release of a game they enjoy, or a food product they already like.

It's something different to do with their time, something to talk about afterwards that makes them feel special, and at the time it's both safe and fun ...and they get a reward afterwards, so everyone's happy!

Recruiting qualitative research using quantitative models and tools

Qualitative and quantitative research are very different disciplines. As we have discussed, qual is never intended to be statistically correct or representative of any demographic segment; its role instead is to explore, in depth, issues and feelings relative to the defined area of interest under consideration.

This couldn't be more different from statistical research... however when it comes to recruitment for qualitative research, it is not unusual to find a desire expressed to use quantitative tools as part of the selection or filtering process.

One regular incidence of this is the use of bespoke

algorithms to define segments or personas. Many of these are proprietary tools, which were developed in secret by brands and their partner agencies often over many years.

They know their customers from extensive quantitative profiling, and desire to model them in order to predict future behaviour.

These can indeed be used in qualitative recruitment, but the ease of doing so depends greatly on the complexity and secrecy of the algorithm. Often we are handed what are effectively black-box tools, usually in the form of a spreadsheet with a locked macro. It consists of a series of questions, for which you input the answers on the spreadsheet, and a result it is spat out: *"The person providing these responses is a typical fit for the 'yellow' profile"*

There are many issues for us doing recruitment using this approach. That's not to say it can't be done, but it can be more difficult than first expected.

Part of the issue is with the secrecy, when we have no idea what defines a 'yellow' persona as opposed to a red blue or green one. Of course we would love to sign your client's NDA and be told a little bit more about it, if we possibly can. This might seem an unusual request from your recruitment partner but it is exceptionally valuable as a sense check – our outlook on the process is qualitative after all.

If blue segment users are supposed to be late technology adopters, innately conservative, family life-stage people – we might find it valuable to know this and compare with other answers given in recruitment, and with what else we know about the applicant based on their previous projects and their membership profile on the Saros database.

Algorithms are not fool-proof, people are not personas, and it is our job to get a rounded qualitative sense of the individual's likely fit in relation to the profile for which we are recruiting.

This is particularly important because very often we know these algorithms are worked out based on data from vast quantitative sources. This data must have contained atypical responses and margins of error – it's a tendency towards a persona, rather than a description of a unique individual.

If we were recruiting you a panel of 2000 people and we ran them all through the algorithm, there is a good chance we would end up with a panel that contained a lot of people who strongly fit the algorithm and embodied the persona.

The panel would also contain extremes who were less of a fit in some ways than others, but still scraped through the scoring process – probably clustered in the kind of bell curve that the stattos would love. Work you did with that panel would, over time, balance out any discrepancies provided by these outliers who less typified the persona – simply because of the scale involved.

However, in qualitative research we might be recruiting you a single focus group of eight people. It is essential therefore that we know a little bit more about what is going on 'under the hood' of the algorithm tool, that we understand the thinking behind using this segmentation as part of the qualitative selection process. Because otherwise if we come across an outlier who nevertheless screens in, there is every chance we will end up recruiting somebody who is perhaps completely wrong for your project – and we won't even know why.

There are often practical issues associated with

applying algorithms in use as well, not least because they frequently involve large numbers of questions.

If we can be provided with the right to unlock the algorithm and see the coding behind it, we may be able to incorporate it into our online screener – use it as part of our pre-filtering, and make sure that we are in fact only calling people who type out strongly as a yellow. This means that we can then focus during our interview on the description of the yellow persona, the softer intangible qualities, and making sure that we recruit people who are the best possible candidates for your research.

When we are provided with a locked tool, the only thing we can do is apply it after the event during the telephone interview stage – this is more cumbersome and expensive, because it does not enable us to rule out those who don't fit before the calling stage.

Depending on the expected incidence of the desired segment(s), the strike rate – and therefore the costs involved in recruitment – may even approach that of cold-calling. This is often a surprise to clients, but it is a consequence of trying to use quantitative tools in qualitative research.

Another way in which statistical models are sometimes applied in recruitment criteria is the use of demographic segmentations, such as the MOSAIC and ACORN profiles.

This is typically something that comes up in publicly funded projects, where resources have been specifically allocated to provide support to particular sections of the community that are perceived as having particular needs or attributes.

Once again, they are essentially quantitative tools, and we run into the dangers of over-generalisation. A specific postal sector in a particular city may be defined as meeting a particular category within the MOSAIC framework, but that postal sector may contain several thousand dwellings, and within that a huge range of different kinds of households and lifestyles.

This is particularly the case in London, which is hugely diverse in sociological composition within very small areas. It's also very problematic in areas of lots of new build and development: planning laws often require mixed tenure in such developments, which completely randomises these profiles – pepper-potting social housing in amongst large privately-owned homes for example, making it impossible to generalise about the demographics of a given street, never mind a larger area.

New developments also remind us that areas change. And statistical models don't always change quickly enough to keep up with them. Remember that the UK Census takes place only once a decade, rather a long time in research, and it takes time for that massive data to filter through to those updating the tools.

According to ACORN data on the last home I bought in the UK, I am highly likely to be a C2 empty nester – which is way off the mark. Yet it probably described a couple of our neighbours and the couple we bought the house from.

What it failed to reflect was a rapidly changing demographic in the area due in part to some excellent Ofsted reports in two local schools, which was causing an influx of young families to increasingly displace the right-to-buy generation who previously had typified the locality – and as such the ACORN description of the area did not match the reality at all.

So it's not surprising that we have had one or two projects of note where we have recruited as instructed based on models like these, carefully checking participant's postcodes against databases, only to find that people don't type out quite as expected. *"You recruited me a load of posh hipsters, who know nothing about the area and have only been here 5 minutes!"* is a response I recall, from a recruit focussed on an inner London segment a few years back.

The area wasn't officially gentrified yet, there were still whole streets without a coffee shop boasting flat whites – but a significant proportion of the people who screened in to the project were indeed not quite the area's original occupants, certainly not of a decade past.

Had the researcher told us they were keen to speak to people who were experiencing change and demographic shift in the area where they'd grown up, we'd have written a very different screener to the one that was approved. We'd not have drawn the lines so tightly on the map, and worked with attitudinal questions as well, to explore the issues our client was really interested in.

On the second round we did exactly this, and found some gems of respondents with fantastic stories to tell. The researcher was very pleased with the recruit – but when we ran the data afterwards to check, it turned out that barely half of them were drawn from the specific postcodes initially specified by MOSAIC – some were just a few streets away, where things were moving at a slower pace, but turned out to be exactly what the researcher wanted.

This salutary tale reminds us of the fact that qual and quant are two very different disciplines.

Using one to recruit the other is a process that has to be done gently and appropriately, not with the bluntness of a sledgehammer. Being able to describe a target recruit in qualitative terms is always the best way to ensure a good fit for a qualitative recruit to go well, and we can use the statistical tools and models as a framework to check things against rather than to be tied to rigidly to the detriment of a good recruit.

Recruiting based on class and social grading

Back when I started work as a street and phone recruiter for quantitative and qualitative research in the previous century, applying strict socioeconomic grading criteria to all participants was a normal and regular part of every interview. Actually, when I first started to do this it was so long ago that we were instructed to grade on the 'head of the household' – defined as the male partner in every case. The idea of the female partner being the chief wage earner, or any household having a structure other than man and his wife, was not really considered.

Not long afterwards it became common practice to apply social grading criteria to the chief wage earner (CWE) in any given household, regardless of their age or sex. Defining a household was occasionally more complex than it sounded but there are careful rules available within the Market Research Society occupational groupings book, which help to make sense of it all – although the criteria for 'relationship' sometimes implies that it is more important whether people sleep together than whether they buy their groceries together.

This underlines the difficulty inherent in trying to classify people based on what sort or class of household or consumer they are. Researchers need to be able to generalise, to categorise, even in qualitative research but to do so meaningfully and fairly is far more of a minefield than it might first appear - not least because of the ways work has changed in recent years.

The ABC1C2DE classification divides people into manual and non-manual workers as an indicator both of education and likely earning power – and for many decades offered a pretty valid heuristic for dividing a population firstly in half, and then into more granular classifications. The theory being, if you work with your brains rather than your hands, that means you are a 'higher class' of consumer.

This classification system is still used of course, but the proportions of people falling into each segment have changed radically. Also, the validity of these classifications in determining likely attitudes and behaviour has also changed.

Manual occupations and careers continue to disappear in the UK at an ever-increasing speed along with the industries that created them. Meanwhile, the C1 classification now encompasses a staggering range of industry sectors, occupations, incomes and levels of responsibility and does not come with any assumptions about level of education or years' work experience.

For example, one of the ways we typically allocated people to either a B or C1 category was the number of subordinates they supervised directly - but these days, work has changed and organisational hierarchies have changed – flattening and becoming more matrix-like. A sales executive might earn huge amounts of commission every month, operating alone on behalf of whichever company has most recently head-hunted their talents – but regardless of their income and perks, they grade out as a C1. Or a technical specialist, in command of huge budgets and procurement decision-making scope, but not having a team under them. A couple of decades ago they'd have had a secretary or two at least, and as such been managers of someone, probably boosting them up to a B.

Managing resources is not seen to be as prestigious as managing people – so they share a socioeconomic grade with a call centre operative working in conditions that have been described as 'white-collar factories', earning barely minimum wage making cold-calls or crunching insurance quotes and getting penalised for going to the bathroom too often.

Outsourcing and self-employment are other factors that have altered forever the way many industries are structured, particularly since the economic crisis and recovery. One side-effect when whole departments are closed with a round of redundancies followed by the same people sometimes being hired to work freelance in similar roles for their previous employers, has been to distort traditional definitions of socioeconomic grading based on occupation!

If that person used to be a product manager heading up a team, but is now performing an identical role as an external consultant, they might even be supervising the old team and also earning a higher hourly rate – but if all of that team are also self-employed consultants hired on a piecework basis, the product manager does not have line-management responsibility for them personally, and he has moved from B to C1 status – regardless of whether he is now earning more or less over an average year.

Freelancing and consultancy mean that many of the highest earners are now subject to quite variable incomes as a result. Perceptions of work-life balance also come into play here. Previous assumptions tended to assume that the chief wage-earner in a household worked an employed full-time job. They stayed within a fairly defined professional path, making moves upwards in income and responsibility at a predictable rate, until cashing out with a final salary pension at the end of it all.

Retired people are graded on their most recent job for this reason, as it is assumed to be their most senior and the pinnacle of their professional life. Portfolio careers, unpaid internships, consulting or simply choosing to take sabbaticals and work fewer hours, were unlikely to have been considered before an era of lifestyle design and flexible working. There is no way to take account of those who can afford to step off the rat race and work more flexibly, despite the fact that they might well only be able to do so because of high level professional qualifications and hourly rates. The underlying assumption is that because they command that status in their official title, they perform at that rate for 40 hours a week, 48 weeks per year. Work is different now, and classification of participants needs to change to reflect that.

The distinguishing features of As B's and C1s are made even more hazy, because they are based not only on numbers of staff line-managed but also qualifications, and certain types of industry are deemed more 'professional' than others. If you choose a career that comes with some kind of worshipful or royal society, that worthiness raises your status as a market research participant as well! This reflects not only the expectation that education correlates with income, but the frankly Edwardian assumption that certain occupational roles are the sole preserve of those of certain classes because they are born superior to others!

And in the 21st century, the assumption that final education level correlates with income is also something many hard-up academics might dispute when they look at what their contemporaries in industry are earning.

That is not to say we cannot or will not recruit using socioeconomic grading criteria. Our interviewers are trained to ask the right questions and use the reference material to apply the principles in the book. It is simply to point out that depending on the assumptions behind it, might not get you the expected results.

For example, if we are asked to recruit ABC1s because the researcher or the client expects that to correlate with whether they can afford a product, then we will exclude all the plumbers earning 90 grand a year in cash, and recruit receptionists and teachers instead, who may not have the income required for the high-end product.

In other situations, we've found that the client expects socioeconomic grade to reflect some degree of 'class' or attitude/behaviour that they associate with their customers, or with intelligence and degree of articulateness. From a recruitment point of view, we would prefer to define what those expected attitudes and behaviours are precisely, and then explicitly recruit against them – rather than assume a correlation that may or may not be present.

We appreciate that certain brands have very clear pictures of exactly who represents the ideal customer, and whether this turns out to be what we find or not when we recruit depends on how the recruitment criteria are framed and presented in a screener. It does not necessarily depend on whether the chief wage earner in their household supervises more or fewer than 10 staff directly.

We have had people instruct us to recruit C1s and above because they consider this will get them a more intelligent and articulate respondent, perhaps for a project requiring particularly creative or conceptual ways of thinking about things - but this won't necessarily work, because anyone who works at a desk is a C1... and we've all come across plenty people of widely varying intellectual capacities who fit this definition, not to mention highly smart and intelligent people who have chosen to work with their hands instead. It would be better to review the chapters on screening for imagination, and work with us to develop screening questions to address the specific kinds of intelligence required to make an effective participant for the project in question.

A further problem relates to seniority in non-manual professions, because we have frequently run into difficulties when asked to recruit mature C2Ds, people close to retirement age. If somebody works in a manual trade all their life, they probably started off as a D then serve an apprenticeship and spend a lot of their career grading as a C2, representing a wide range of experience and expertise levels.

Once they have served a few decades in this trade it is highly likely they will attain other responsibilities including management and supervisory ones, which actually push them to C1 status. If they have the advanced skills required to be a high-level C2, they only have to start supervising a small team of others to move up in grading, so recruiting a group of C2 respondents in their 50s and 60s can be almost impossible, going by the book definition of their social grade.

Despite the decline in UK manufacturing industry it is still possible to recruit a group of participants in their 50s and 60s who have worked in manual occupations all of their lives, and probably are strongly representative of the desired community – they just probably won't still officially be C2Ds by the time they are approaching their gold pocket watch.

But with all of the above said however, recruiting via socioeconomic grading according to the MRS definitions is actually more straightforward than applying criteria which simply state 'working' or 'middle' or 'upper' or 'lower' class.

So, which are you anyway? …Yes we do see this from time to time, sometimes on briefs from clients outside of the UK, sometimes on briefs from clients with little background in the research industry.

The bottom line is, we are not going to write a screening question with a closed-response question asking people whether they are Cleese, Barker or Corbett!

What we have to do instead is have a frank conversation about the thinking that inspired this, and drill down into criteria against which we can actually screen and recruit.

It might be as simple as income – the client just means they want to speak to people with an average or above average household income, who are the most likely to be in the market for the consumer electronics product they are thinking of launching.   In that case we can ask about household income in the screener, or perhaps even more effectively we can ask about typical spending on goods in this category, because the amount of income alone does not determine this given widely varying commitments and priorities in domestic spending.

This factor is further confounded by regional variances in cost of living, which can be particularly pronounced within parts of the UK.

How much you earn does not necessarily dictate how much you have to spend on discretionary things – but the latter can be screened for in recruitment.

At other times we have determined that it is really about

perception as to a typical customer and their degree of 'style' or 'class' ...how that brand perceives itself to rank amongst others in the category – who their competitors are. This might be informed by detailed and up-to-date quantitative brand tracking, or it might be a quaint and wistful assumption of the founder – either way, we are far more likely to recruit the people you want if you describe them to us in a descriptive pen-portrait manner from which we can extrapolate appropriate screening questions.

If it turns out in recruitment that the product really is a huge favourite of builders' wives rather than Sloane Rangers, we will have to have a discussion – see the chapter on unexpected screen-outs. If you are working on the assumption that occupation or current gross income will directly correlate with intelligence, imagination or being articulate, then I'd suggest that is actually hugely tenuous as assumptions go. You would probably end up with a better quality recruit by considering the specific attributes and attitudes you need participants to exhibit, and screening against those deliberately.

Recruiting projects which are "market research mixed with something else"

Sometimes we are asked to recruit research participants for an exercise in which some elements definitely fall outside of the Code of Conduct. They might not be ethically wrong, and the majority of the exercise may indeed clearly meet the definitions of research – however there is something about it that takes a step outside the safeguards of the code and the usual industry parameters.

This does not mean that we cannot recruit it or that we will decline to do so. However, we may require that additional safeguards and conditions are put in place to ensure the well-being of the participants we recruit at every level.

An example of this might be a group discussion that will take place in the normal way, and be filmed directly at the viewing facility. The client then wants to use footage from this film in marketing materials later on, so this element is outside of research uses. Another project might involve recruitment of a citizen's jury to spend a day workshopping an aspect of social policy in their region, a valid and worthwhile research exercise – however for the last half-hour of the workshop they are to be joined by government ministers and an associated press pack likely to be seeking quotes and vox pops from participants. This last is highly likely to compromise their anonymity.

In this event we will first make certain we completely understand exactly what is going to be required of participants, including requesting sight of any releases that they will be asked to sign, in respect of how footage and recordings may be used.   We will then be completely transparent with participants at the point of initial invitation to apply, explaining exactly what they would be getting involved with, and which elements are market research and which are not.

In most cases, with projects of this nature, it would not be practical or possible for them to take part in only the confidential research aspects – so they need to understand that involvement with any of it means involvement with all of it. Organisers of the policy workshop really do not want to have participants exercising their right to leave just before the PR bit takes place. Our interviewer will probe and make certain that applicants are completely comfortable with all of this, before booking them into the project.

Usually at this stage to we would want to negotiate some extra incentive payment for those taking part, to motivate them to apply, but also to acknowledge that what the client will gain from them goes beyond the usual limits. If you are getting material for a training video or conference presentation at the same time as running a focus group then that hopefully represents a saving to you - some of this should be passed on to the participants whose identity and images will be used for your additional benefit.

Hybrid projects of this nature require very careful consideration and individual assessment, to decide whether we will recruit them at all. A lot comes down to which elements of the code may be compromised, because people may be able to give informed consent to giving up their anonymity, but they can never be asked to consent to be harmed or suffer adverse consequences. These consequences might not be immediately obvious, but it is our job to make sure they are pre-empted.

As an example, we were once asked to recruit participants with subclinical raised cholesterol levels, to take part in trials of a food designed to help lower their cholesterol. The project included having tests at the beginning and end of the trial. All parties knew that it was a PR exercise not a clinical trial, and this was a food product already licensed and sold, not a pharmaceutical product. So everything seemed fine... until the researcher asked us to ask the participants to eat an especially hearty breakfast before the baseline measurement, deliberately raising their cholesterol for the first test! Bear in mind these were people who had already received a warning about their levels from their GP – they were not so seriously ill as to require medication, but they had been specifically told to change their lifestyle to avoid this.

Was it ethical for us to ask them to explicitly contravene their doctor's instructions just for one morning? We felt that this instruction crossed the line – fine for these ladies to take part in the photo session and press interviews if they were happy to do so, but their blood chemistry would have to stand without undue influence.

We have also recruited a number of other interesting projects at the boundaries of science and market research, involving monitoring biological and neurological responses to different images used in advertising, or research involving the use of virtual reality headsets.

Again our approach is to ask lots of questions to establish firmly that participants will suffer no detriment, beyond possibly having to wipe a dollop of conductive gel from their temples on completion, and to make sure that we are able to answer any questions from potential participants that might arise during recruitment.

This kind of project has never been a problem to recruit because the equipment involved has already passed safety trials before coming to market, and also because the right participants are absolutely fascinated by what they will have to do. How much more interesting, to respond to virtual stimulus in 3-D, than something glued to a pasteboard in a viewing facility!

No enhanced incentives needed here, and it's actually a positive, distinguishing thing we can use creatively in recruitment to encourage people to apply - but we might need to pre-screen for anyone suffering from vertigo or claustrophobia or epilepsy, in order to be certain they cannot be harmed in any way by their participation so, as ever, we need to know exactly what is going to happen in the session.

Some of the things we are asked to quote for have nothing to do with research whatsoever, such as people asking us to recruit social media advocates or reviewers, or quiz show participants. These are easy to identify and decline. It's the ones that are mostly a good bona fide research exercise blended subtly with a bit of something else, which require the most careful assessment.

Issues in Recruitment

Of course, we all hope that your recruitment project goes exactly as you expect – but working with real people as we all do, unexpected issues can arise occasionally and need dealing with. Finding effective solutions to challenges, still delivering great recruitment on time and on budget, is all part of the fun.

Nobody is Eligible! Dealing with Unexpected Screen Outs.

One thing that can derail a project in dramatic fashion is every potential applicant screening out.   Or far more people screening out than we expected at a particular point.

Now, every question in every screener has the effects of filtering out non-eligible applicants, and it is our job as recruiters to make sure we pass sufficient numbers of people through it to make the recruit itself viable. When we are designing this screener in the first place we naturally have a fairly good idea of whether this is going to represent a high or low incidence recruit – indeed this will be reflected in the initial costings and timelines that we agree, because the specified participants might be either fairly general or they might be incredibly niche. Niche is fine, provided the niche fundamentally exists – and this is where occasionally we may run into difficulties.

Whether we have costed and accepted the work as a highly-niche best-odds project or not, sometimes we simply find a single question is ruling out practically every applicant in a way we hadn't expected. Something unusual is going on, which definitely bears a closer look…

Perhaps it is the way the question is worded, some nuance to the language that we had all missed, something that turns out to be more value-laden that we had anticipated. Perhaps there might be some ambiguity to the meaning of the question, which means that people are unclear which way to go.

Sometimes there might be difficulty with honesty or disclosure, if we are asking about something very embarrassing, or possibly illegal. We know that a certain proportion of the people to whom we are sending the screener definitely exhibit this behaviour and, by extension, a proportion of those completing it must do as well - and if they don't want to admit it in a screener, then they certainly won't want to discuss it in a group.

What can we do in this case to make it easier and safer for them to confess whatever it is? One case of a project of this nature was about illegal downloading of movies and music, and we ended up having to explain in the screener and invitation that we were excluding all members of the legal, police, or any other professions as potential applicants. People would not comfortable even revealing that they did something which could potentially attract massive fines, even though we all knew that it was not uncommon behaviour.

It was interesting in that case that people trusted the research process to protect their anonymity – they just didn't necessarily trust their fellow participants. This was one of those cases such as were discussed under 'sensitive recruitment' above, where it is actually far more effective to be completely transparent about the subject and behaviour of interest, and simply ask directly about it.

This produced far better results than trying to hide the behaviour that interested us most amongst a load of general statements about media consumption, a screener through which nobody tended to disclose any dodgy behaviour at all, and it also meant that the researcher was able to get straight to the heart of their discussion quickly without too many barriers on the night.

Occasionally the question eliminating everybody will be one that we simply did not see coming, because it relates to something specific about the recruit that we are not aware of, such as recruiting users of a relatively new app, which has no penetration data available. We won't shy away from taking the recruit on even if nobody in the office has heard of this product, but perhaps once we get it out there we will find out that nobody outside of our office has heard of it either, and then we have a problem. Perhaps this one could be solved by using customer lists from the client themselves, if they really want to be certain they are talking to genuine users of their product.

From a project management point of view, we are very clear that it will not help you as the recruitment supplier for us just to go back to you and say, *"We cannot find anybody that fits."* That won't help you to help us, or to help your client (internal or external) get what they need. We would much rather help identify some way to make the project doable, and one way we can tackle this is to look at the results together. While we never cease to remind people that qual and quant are very different beasts, in the early stages of screening at least, you can take something of a more quantitative view, looking at the data. We are very happy to strip out the sensitive contact information and send you that data to look at directly. If we have 400 results, and all but two of them are screening out on question 8C, then question 8C is clearly where we need to focus our attention.

We will also have a close look at those two people who have screened through okay, because there might be something they have in common, which we can better leverage in future recruitment. If you ask us to recruit users of a niche skincare brand, ranging in age from 30 to 55, and we screen out hundreds of people only to find that the only people using it are 50 or older, then that is something we will need to discuss with you urgently. It might be that the user profile is different from that which your client expected, but we could still find two groups of users provided we focus our efforts on the older age segment – quit throwing the screener at younger people, who are ticking all the wrong brands and screening out.

At least in this scenario we know that two of them are a perfect fit for your project, so that proves these people exist, and theoretically if we can target it right we ought to be able to recruit the rest of them (though this is subject to constraints such as the size of our database and lead time we have on the project).

More worrying is when we are looking at hundreds of responses but nobody fits, and that is something we will need to look at very urgently, and with your help because unfortunately it is rarely as simple as *'change question 8C and everything will fall into place overnight'*. We will need to work together to look at the quantitative results with more qualitative eyes – so, it turns out that the pre-family applicants are less likely to agree strongly with the attitude statement, even though they are using more of the preferred brands.

Perhaps if we flex on the attitude statement slightly or agree to prove that with some variations in the telephone screening, we alter the target quota for the family versus pre-family split.   Or perhaps it would simply be helpful to offer some lunchtime sessions as well as evening, if we want young mums to be free to attend?

The issue of timing or logistical reasons for the screen-out is one which can never be overlooked, because sometimes the situation is actually far simpler to resolve than we had anticipated. We once found that swapping a men's and women's groups over in the schedule removed a clash with a football match that a lot of people regarded as particularly important and had a disproportionate attraction for research participants of the male persuasion.

Another time we found out that a particular medication was mainly used by people who were older than we'd realised, and had difficulties getting to the venue – a bit of rethinking on the timing and locations was all that was needed to make the project recruitable after all.

What we need from you as our clients is a willingness to accept that if we run into unexpected screen-out difficulties, this is actually a research finding in its own right – as opposed to our failure to find the right people yet. We know our database, we know where it is weak or strong, and if we say to you there is a real problem with this set of questions then that is honestly where the problem lies, as opposed to our being lazy or the right people not having clicked through.

We fully appreciate how difficult it is for you to go back to your client at this point and say, *"Hey folks we have a problem..."* – which is why we fully collaborate with you, coming up with a range of possible options that will still lead to the research objectives of the client being fulfilled – even if it is not going to happen in exactly the way we all expected at the beginning.

We will come into the conference call with your clients and explain directly if that's helpful – we'd far rather the people you are working for were open to hearing about the problems directly and see us as part of the team dedicated to helping them get what they need from the research, as opposed to some useless and intransigent supplier only interested in doing what is easy and straightforward.

We can share the data with them as well and look at it together, this has sometimes led to some quite serendipitous new directions for the research – like a client glancing at a bunch of answers, and saying, *"That's not what we expected, but it's really interesting... please can you arrange for us to talk to that person!"*

Because we work flexibly at Saros we are used to working in a highly consultative way with many of our associates, we would rather be your partner in fieldwork, sharing responsibility for coming up with creative solutions, than somebody working at arm's length with a fixed brief and incomplete information. This is one more reason that we ask you to tell us as much as possible about the background, to project what your client is trying to achieve in the long term, the history that led up to this specific fieldwork exercise, and any particular difficulties experience with research recruitment in the past. The more we know, the more helpful we can be, and the better we can bring our experience to bear on similar challenges.

The converse is also true of course. If we find ourselves working for somebody who says, in so many words, "I don't care, that's your problem, just find people who fit," – then there is very little we can do to move things forward. We have even occasionally had people say to us, *"Find people who SAY they fit, who will look and sound as if they fit, for 2 hours next Thursday!"*

This is obviously our worst case scenario from a recruitment point of view, because we will have to say that there is nothing more we can do. While being flexible on every factor we will never ask people to lie about anything to take part in research. That's a line we won't cross, and reflects one of the very few circumstances we have ever had to walk away from a job mid-way through it.

Certainly, in most cases, unexpected screen-outs are simply part of the challenge of working with interesting and demanding recruitment briefs. A niche recruit is expected to be low incidence and we allow for the fact that it will take more time and resources to complete, but the unexpected is just that and usually means that between us we have failed to anticipate or allow for some factor either intrinsic to the project itself or in the wider environment... So long as we can approach it as a shared challenge with a collaborative solution, there will be one way or another we can get it resolved between us.

Professional and Serial Respondents

It's time to talk openly about something that all too often gets kicked back under the rug – but has to be addressed in any book about recruiting participants for paid research.

For a long time, the issue of fraudulent recruitment was qualitative research's dirty secret, perhaps more so in the UK than anywhere else. Many researchers may have felt uncomfortable with some of the participants they met in their groups, particularly if they met a few of them far too often... but with such a small pool of recruiters available in certain areas, there was a definite avoidance and unwillingness to confront difficulties. We know these difficulties amounted to outright corruption in some instances. Things are definitely different now, but there is still relatively little open discussion of the problem within the industry.

While any researcher with a shred of professional pride chose not to work with recruiters they knew to be 'bent', they were not in a position to know how many of their recruited participants were, or were not, who they were supposed to be - because there are two levels at which research participant fraud can potentially occur: A recruiter can lie about who they are recruiting and even collude with participants to deceive, or a recruiter can be deceived by people happy to lie to them, in order to get into paid-research events.

So far as the recruitment end of it goes, it's easy to see how such behaviours arose, when both budgets and timeframes have always been tighter than anyone would choose. As discussed earlier, doing recruitment the traditional way, going out and finding fresh people each time and then trying to screen them into your project is unrealistically difficult. Research procurers haven't always been ready to listen to those difficulties and negotiate pragmatically about what may or may not be flexed upon. Indeed, it's fair to say that in some instances there has arisen a 'conspiracy of silence'... *"Just make sure there are people who look like a great fit on the night, so I look good in front of my client, and we'll say no more."*

Recruitment briefs have always clearly stated that you cannot recruit people known to you, or people who have taken part within the past 6 months, and that's crucial. If someone was collecting notes about past respondents in a little black book or whatever, there was probably no other way to fulfil challenging recruitment briefs before the internet and extensive databases existed. If you decide you are going to break the rules about those one or two points, it's the top of a slippery slope; you'd then have to collude also with the participants themselves – *"if anybody asks you, you've never done this kind of thing before, OK!"* Doubtless it could fast become a mutually beneficial relationship where a recruiter has a small team of folks they know are reliable and effective participants and sends them out far too often, to different projects and researchers. Of course, from telling lies about how often they've taken part, it's a relatively easy and natural progression, to start negotiating other recruitment criteria as well.

Although small in number, fraudulent collaborative recruiters exist, and as word gets around, respectable researchers simply avoid working with them – the problem is hopefully self-limiting.

A different kind of problem however arises when research

participants set out deliberately to deceive recruiters. To try and maximise their own income as research participants by lying about everything from their identity to their participation history.

You can google it, there are plenty of anonymous articles around, about how to 'make a living' bluffing your way into research events. Every researcher we have spoken to has come across one or more of these deceitful characters in their career... Faces that just look a bit too familiar, answers a little too pat, maybe just a blatant contradiction, which amounts to at least one outright lie – because when you met that guy 3 weeks ago in a different viewing facility, they had a different occupation and drove a different car.

We KNOW these people exist, and we know they're probably all on our database. We believe they are relatively small in number, compared with the proportional impact they have on our industry and, knowing exactly who many of them are, have tagged them already. We won't have every single one of them and are not afraid to admit the truth.

We advertise openly and regularly for new participants to register with us, so why wouldn't they respond? We also know they'll quickly be disappointed when they realise we enforce the '6-month exclusion' rule pretty tightly, and won't be party to sending them out to projects every week by way of a part time job. Their earning potential through Saros is unfortunately going to be very limited, and probably compares badly to other sources that are less picky about such matters.

We have even spoken with people who seem genuinely surprised to learn that the industry frowns upon weekly participation. They can't believe we don't have something for them to take part in just because they call up and ask for it – they are either incredibly naive, collusive fraudsters of the kind described above, or they might simply have worked with an unscrupulous recruiter who kept careful records of clients to whom they were sent on a rotating basis.

They're disappointed to discover that things are different with us, but obviously it's very helpful when they identify themselves to us so clearly and distinctly, and we're able to get them tagged before sending them anywhere near one of our clients.

They might already have plenty going on through these other companies and give up on us, or they might develop 'Participant Multiple Personality Disorder', and decide to create repeat profiles on our database. We are often quite astonished at the lengths to which people go to populate these fictitious personas, because quite a lot of work is clearly involved on their part. No wonder they regard it as a part-time business or job…

Almost every day we catch people trying to register with us using a combination of contact or profiling information, which is already in use on our database. This prompts closer examination by human intervention. Sometimes it's a person re-registering in error, perhaps after many years and a change of job or address. At other times it's definitely a lot more suspicious. Without going into detail about our de-duplication tools and routines, I can state that it is difficult to make a completely fresh and unique set of data. Some attempts are clumsy and blatantly false. Others are a bit subtler and show a lot of effort – we once found 9 'different' women in a small Midlands city who shared a set of initials and a mobile phone number, despite the fact that they all had different addresses, jobs, email addresses, dates of birth etc.

It gives our database administration team a great sense of satisfaction to bust one of these multifaceted characters; not that we claim international espionage professional-level identity checking – this is market research not an episode of Spooks. We do recognise that we cannot stop people fooling us completely in this very elaborate way if they manage to create a profile that at a glance seems totally unique. It won't get them into more than one project every 6 months at the absolute best, so very few people bother.

It isn't particularly in their interests to do so. Once we identify them as a 'groupie' we rarely confront them (unless caught in the act) – instead we quietly tag them with our suspicions, and no longer have any suitable projects coming up to tempt them.

After all, the last thing we need is their creating yet another profile.

Our experienced interviewers are also quick at spotting those who are clearly trying to game the system. Writing good screening questions as discussed above is one way to make sure people don't know what answers to give but often you can spot somebody who is trying to be all things to all people in their responses, avoid any typical screen-outs (and clearly know what to look for).

Even on the phone they can give themselves away through use of inappropriate terminology – somebody who says they have never taken part in research before, but starts asking about incentive payments and viewing facilities... they are heading straight for a conversation ending, *"Unfortunately the specific combination of responses you have given both online and on the phone mean that you are not a match for our client's requirements on this occasion, thank you very much for your interest in taking part in our research."*

So while recognising that these people are a problem for our industry and also directly attempting to infiltrate our database, it might seem that we award them relatively little importance in our daily work. We just tag, isolate and move on – because we firmly believe that the best way to mitigate their impact is to avoid and ignore them.

We prefer instead to try and crush them with sheer numbers of real participants.

How many 'groupies' are there out there? Nobody knows – maybe a few hundred, in the UK. We proceed with our containment measures daily, which include sharing information discreetly with trusted competitors, as well as acting on tip-offs from clients and research facilities.

There are creative ways to work within the constraints of data protection law, but improve data quality. Bearing in mind that we rarely actually meet the participants we recruit face-to-face, intelligence received from those who do so is extremely helpful. We have even been forwarded stills from viewing facility recordings on occasion to help confirm that one person really is using two identities. Nobody in our industry likes a cheat, and researchers who use our services regularly have a vested interest in helping us keep our database clean and clear of crooks, likewise the people who provide other services to the research industry.

We devote far greater resources and attention to recruiting new potential participants instead, reaching out to and registering completely fresh people who have never taken part in research before at any time. They are our best weapon against the groupies, drowning out the false personas and opinions that make a mockery of everything the qualitative research industry is trying to accomplish.

There are far more real people out there than fakes, and they have so much to bring to fieldwork, with fresh ideas and ways of looking at things, and they interest us much more than a relatively small number of liars and cheats.

Smooth and Successful Fieldwork

Participant Profiles and Documents

Although the product you are buying from us is successful face to face fieldwork, one of your first tangible outputs of the process will be the participant profile documents that are sent to you, usually a few days before your research starts (if we send it too early, you can bet there will be revisions as drop-outs are replaced)

We have standard templates for presenting this information, which we have designed to give you a single-sheet overview of the people you are meeting – something you can hand to your client as well, if they are watching an interview or discussion live. Our intention is to summarise the criteria and responses at a group/quota as well as individual level, to make it easy to identify quickly who is who and why they have been chosen to participate.

You might have a different way in which you prefer this information to be presented, and that's great – we would simply ask that the earlier in the recruitment process you can provide your template for this, the better we can align the ways we collect and collate the information to best suit your needs. Ideally we will design this spreadsheet alongside the design of the screener, creating a consistent and unified process. We hope that by this point we have a clear idea of which are your most important recruitment criteria, also which criteria show meaningful variation between one participant and another – as opposed to the fact that they are all female or all vegetarian or whatever. We will try to use the space in your profile document to highlight the differences of interest.

As a general rule when using our own template, the profiles you receive will not contain any contact information for participants. They will be identified by first name only, along with age and occupation first name and initial if there are duplicates; we did once manage to recruit a focus group of eight people containing five named Clare, but that is unusual... the researcher said it would have made his life a lot easier if we'd actually made all the rest of them 'Clares' too, but that was not in the brief.

We know that clients like to see these documents, and we also know that they can get printed out multiple times, and left behind in viewing facilities and so on. Whilst we collect permission from every participant we recruit to pass their contact number on to you for use on the night, we do not routinely include these details in profiling documents for that reason – we don't want you worrying about having to collect and shred every copy of it at the end of a long night of fieldwork. We would prefer to supply that list separately for your viewing facility receptionist or host to make use of in case there are any non-arrivals.

Similarly, we are happy to supply a list including surnames, where this is required for logistical reasons – for example when somebody has to sign in to a secure building in order to reach a research facility. But this identifying data cannot be given to your client or anybody else, without breaching the Code of Conduct.

Incidentally if the location is so secure that particular proof of identity will be required, we definitely need to know this in advance so that we can advise participants both on the phone and in writing, and make sure they show up with whatever documents are required. It's rarely an issue at research viewing facilities, but we know that research can sometimes take place in offices sharing reception access to all other areas with more sensitive controls in place.

Going forward from the discussion above about participants who are not who they claim to be, we know that some recruitment companies routinely ask people anyway to bring along ID. This is not a route we have decided to go down from our own point of view, but if you would prefer participants to bring documents to confirm their identity then we will simply advise this in their joining details. We will need clear instructions from you as to what ID is acceptable, for example must it contain a photo, or it must it be primary ID, not routinely carried by most people in the UK (unlike in many other countries) even a driving licence may not be carried around daily by somebody working in central London.

The reason we don't make this part of our general joining instructions is simply due to an underlying assumption that people are who they claim to be. We ensure through our processes that there is no significant advantage to them in lying about their identity, nor about other factors they think will make them better able to qualify for the research (when they don't know what those factors are anyway)

If there is a research-based reason why they should have to confirm such things then that's of course different – so if we were recruiting a project that involved testing alcohol, then it would be absolutely reasonable to request that they brought primary ID referencing their date of birth. This is in exactly the same category of reasoning that would require somebody to bring along the logbook for the car featured in research, or the mobile phone they are going to test apps for. Not because we expect them to have lied to us, but because if there is any confusion or ambiguity here they will not be eligible or able to participate meaningfully in the research at all.

Apart from that, we start with the premise that the participants we recruit are responsible, truthful and well-behaved adults. This almost always turns out to be the case. I visited a viewing facility once that had a statement of participant responsibilities on the wall, including the advice that anyone perceived to be under the influence of drink or drugs would be ejected from the premises and not entitled to an incentive. I could not help but feel that to state this somehow raises an expectation that it could happen, that it must have happened before, and that this is a way in which a proportion of people are expected to behave.

Out of the many thousands of people we have sent along to research events over the years, we have heard the occasional extraordinary anecdote about people turning up unfit to participate for various unlikely reasons, but most researchers and facilities we work with are not in need of special guidance as to how this should be dealt with, being quite comfortable to apply common sense and judgement to each situation as it arises.

Participants and Non-Participants Feedback

Which brings us on to that for most group situations, not everybody we recruit will go on to take part in the research

This is exactly what we expect and over-recruit for, because it's essential that your research starts on time with the right number of people. As discussed earlier we might recruit 9,10 or in exceptional circumstances even larger numbers, to ensure your group of eight people is seated in the room when the clock strikes six. When you have those eight in front of you and you are happy to start with the introductions, you probably give little thought to those spares, nor afterwards, when your client is clamouring for your initial thoughts, and you are trying to prepare for the next group starting in 10 minutes' time...

So we apologise for the fact that we will chase you the next day, to try and find out exactly what happened to all 10 of the people we sent you.

Of course if there are sufficient seats then perhaps you went ahead with all 10, got more than you bargained for, and everybody's happy. That's great, we will update our database with the news that all took part.

Perhaps though, somebody rang the viewing facility very late to say they would be late or unable to attend, or worst of all simply didn't bother to show up. That merits an update to our database too... Unless they spontaneously come up with an extremely good excuse, nobody gets to do that to us (or you) twice.

Everybody has our and your phone numbers, multiple email addresses, and points of contact for getting in touch. They are reminded and chased about their participation to the point of irritation for some, so blowing out without a word is simply unacceptable (unless they are abruptly hospitalised or in an accident on the way to the session, which we won't usually find out for a while). So, a no-show means 'never again', and we need to know that.

At other times they might simply be the 9th or 10th person to arrive at the session, punctually, and be told they are too late to take part. For some, receiving their full incentive but able to go straight home again might be perceived as a real result – two hours of their lives they do not have to spend discussing packets of soup.

Some might be, conversely, extremely disappointed having greatly looked forward to their participation. It really is true that people don't just do it for the money. Sometimes we do such a good job persuading them of the significance of their contribution and the influence they will have, to be denied that opportunity is a great let-down.

The thing is, in terms of updating our records the following day, we treat all of these reactions and circumstances very differently. A no-show is removed from the Christmas card list for good, whereas somebody devastatingly disappointed at being turned away, we will do our best to prioritise somehow in future – whilst we have no idea when a suitable project might arise for them, at least we can make sure they get an apology.

We also track people who are paid off in this way quite carefully, just to make certain they don't conclude that arriving a strategic few minutes late in future is an excellent way to take the money and run. Whilst we would normally expect most researchers to pay an incentive in full to anybody arriving within around 15-20 minutes of the start time, we definitely would not let anybody make a habit of this.

Incidentally, we would also really love to know what you thought about the people who did take part.

When we telephone interview everybody before we send them your way, we're realistically spending only a few minutes talking to them compared with the couple of hours you enjoy, and we never see them face-to-face. We hope that most people who take part in your event will get the chance to do so again, in another suitable but quite different project, after a minimum of six months has elapsed.

We know that most people have the potential to be good-enough research participants, but that others are simply star class... They bring something to every conversation and interaction they are part of, which makes them exceptionally effective. They might be perfectly okay most of the time, yet have a particular subject or kind of engagement that really makes them shine and adds incredible levels of value.

If you come across somebody amongst the participants we have sent to you who is exceptional in any way, it is really helpful if you can let us know about it. This lets us tap them for the future in a way that serves our industry in new ways

Occasionally you might come across somebody who for a reason unapparent during recruitment, is not a great respondent.

They might be bored, unwell, or reacting to something in their own life that prevents them from contributing effectively on the night. They might think in a very literal or unimaginative way and cannot cope with some exercises.

Occasionally we have come across somebody who, after a great one-to-one by phone with our interviewer, turns out to be cripplingly shy in a group discussion and utterly unable to contribute. There might be a personal reason but they are just not ideal to be part of a group.

Yes, these factors can be incredibly subjective and judgemental but, bearing in mind that we don't get to see these people and know them in the way you do, it is extremely useful if you feed back to us anything you learn or see about, which might make them more or less suitable for participation in any future event.

We like to think that there is a suitable project out there for every possible participant but perhaps that turns out to be an online study…

Feedback from Participants

As well as chasing you for feedback a day or so after your fieldwork, we also ask participants what they thought about taking part. We like to send them an email to say thank you first of all, but we also want to know their feelings about the whole experience – from their recruitment and involvement with Saros through to the bits we know nothing about, their actual participation itself.

These participant testimonials are very valuable to us from a PR point of view, being as they are overwhelmingly positive and enthusiastic about the events they have just attended. We use them extensively as social proof, including video statements from those happy to provide them. We know that for any project we recruit there will be far more people disappointed and rejected than who go on to take part, this is simply the nature of screening – and it has led to some social media backlashes on occasion, from people who take it personally and who have even accused us of not running paid events at all!

So we love it when real life participants step up and set them straight, sharing their own experiences and perspectives on their participation, and reassuring everybody that there is a genuine paid face-to-face event at the end of every screening process. Anybody looking at our YouTube channel or Facebook page can see that people of all ages and backgrounds and all over the UK take part in our events each week, and are happy to tell the world about it.

The feedback we obtain helps us continually to improve our workflow and the information we provide to those taking part, and helps us to understand what people gain from their participation. This informs our content strategy, and how we develop the messages we use to connect with potential new participants – particularly when they reflect on any concerns or reservations they may have had beforehand, which were overcome during the session.

Our intention is obviously to address such worries beforehand another time, because they are the kind of thing which can potentially provoke a no-show. However, people sometimes feel less comfortable about telling us what concerns them, until they are looking back on the incident and whatever they feared has not come to pass. It also enables us to feed back to clients or venues in the case of any problems.

Such incidents are rare, and many are highly subjective. If, for example, we recruit for discussion groups for one researcher and a single participant tells us that the researcher was rude or unpleasant, this probably says more about the participant than the researcher.

Sometimes feedback only makes sense when compared with that received from other participants or indeed from the moderator, but we can easily identify any common threads emerging, and ensure that these are fed back to those who need to know.

Participants have a strong sense of fair play, and are often sensitive to any perceived favouritism or confirmation bias they pick up. People tell us if they feel that they were not being listened to because their opinions were not what the researcher wanted to hear, or felt that other members of the group were being shut down or overlooked.

Whilst we do receive continual praise and respect for the difficulties and challenges moderators often face, there is little patience with failure to control dominant respondents, or obvious bias in the way a conversation is facilitated. We have had participants say that they felt moved to defend the views of others, or stop personal criticisms that moderator laughed off – it is unusual for anything so unprofessional to be reported, but it has happened. Inexperience or lack of control by the moderator is also perceived extremely negatively, just like a poor junior teacher who dares show a sign of weakness from which the group will not allow them to recover…

Other feedback is more confused than negative per se, such as people who express bafflement about some of the exercises and projective techniques they were involved with; "*I cannot imagine how talking about which kind of animal it would be, can have helped them learn anything about how to rebrand a holiday resort!*"

Of course their role is just to free-associate and work through their responses with the researcher, whose job it is to interpret and analyse and generate meaning from what seems to the individual participant to be totally off-the-wall information. It reminds us that for participants, their interview *is* the research – they don't think about how information is aggregated and analysed and contextualised. It just seems to them that the discussion last night got really weird, and they have no idea why.

Feedback like this helps to remind us how different people are in terms of how they respond to imaginative tasks, indeed there are those who report cringing embarrassment at being asked to do something like a collage or psycho-drawing. Whilst the same exercise might be the highlight of the evening for some participants who love nothing more than getting down and dirty with scissors and glue-stick. Another might state, *"It was awful, I felt like I was back in primary school and I hated it."*

Arguably this is an issue that could easily have been addressed in screening – had we been made aware of the nature of the tasks to be undertaken in the session we simply have included a question to rule out the latter participant as unsuitable. His collage was probably rubbish anyway, so this would have been better for all concerned.

Non-research factors often receive the most detailed feedback, such as reviews about refreshments that would do Giles Coren proud; whatever you do don't stint on the sandwiches! Being presented with decent food has a massive impact on the mind-set and helpfulness of many participants, if they feel welcomed and valued they contribute so much more happily, and it's a small cost difference in comparison to the potential gain.

On the other hand you cannot please all the people all of the time whatever you do, and we have had negative comments about food they were not sure was for them as they were never actually invited to partake of it; others complaining about the lack of catering for special diets, and others blaming us for not telling them exactly what food would be available, so that they could have avoided eating beforehand...

Most damning of all though was the feedback received from a participant glimpsing far higher quality food being delivered to the backroom than that which they were offered...

When it comes to the clients and direct viewing, very few participants remark on this at all.

I think a great many people taking part in research these days are totally comfortable with the idea of being under surveillance and recorded throughout their lives, and give as much thought to this going on in the viewing facility as they give to all the cameras tracking them through the streets as they walked there.

Provided the moderator explains and quickly moves on from the idea of the mirror, it's clear that people forget about this as well, and don't really think about the people watching them.

We've seen clips of participants pausing to check their hair or lipstick, completely forgetting the other use of the strangely grey surface, by the time they come to leave.

Unless of course they are abruptly reminded, such as on one dreadful occasion when a group all clearly heard laughter from the back room while they were discussing embarrassing medical problems ...an incident that effectively ended the discussion early... what could the moderator possibly say after that happened?

Other participants report becoming reminded that it is actually a two-way mirror, because they have glimpsed the flash of a phone screen from behind it – perhaps suggesting to them that they are not being observed very attentively after all.

The viewing facility or venue is often another hygiene factor for the researcher, who visits so many different ones each month, but the for participants the venue forms critical part of the overall experience, and sets the mood for their session from the moment they arrive - sometimes earlier, if it proves difficult to find or get into. Welcoming and friendly reception staff bring praise, as does a comfortable reception area.

One time that viewing facilities can come in for

criticism is tactless handling of late arrivals or surplus participants. If all 10 are there before the start time, then two may need to be paid off and sent away – but how this is done and in front of whom can make all the difference.

Ideally it should be the researcher's choice, because they have the profiles in front of them and are best placed to decide who of 10 they least want in the room – however when they are warming up for a group and particularly if working alone, this is rarely practicable, and the decision tends to fall to a host or reception person at the viewing facility.

If the decision appears to be arbitrary or even consensual – if other participants are aware of it's going on at all – then they all entered the room thinking, *"Hang on, he just got his money and didn't even have to do anything!"* Not the best frame of mind for being a great research participant.

Others have occasionally witnessed what can only be described as altercations, between late participants declined their incentive money or punctual spares devastated at being excluded from the session.

We have found that some facilities do not have senior staff around to cover evening sessions and things can be left with quite junior hosts who are ill-prepared to deal with the occasional strong emotions coming up over the life-or-death issue of market research participation.

As well as procedural things like this, we do pass feedback to facilities on matters like the temperature of the room and the comfort of the seating, because these can make such a difference to how a group goes.

We look for a common thread for consensus and sense whether people are casting around for something to criticise as though it's expected of them. A design company client of ours was thrown into disarray by a statement from a participant regarding the hand dryers in the bathroom, which were actually a test product of theirs, perhaps a little too innovative for that market!

Where a viewing facility is situated is, of course, something nobody there can do much about, but if people report that the place is difficult to find or they feel unsafe leaving after a late session, then we can take this into account when recommending locations for future projects or preparing better joining instructions another time

It is rare however for any negative feedback to be received at all, most people really love being invited to take part in an interesting group that is well managed and moderated.

Often they sound genuinely surprised, perhaps particularly so for projects where the subject matter itself sounds a little mundane and uninspiring. They have perhaps resigned themselves to an evening discussing utility switching or wallpaper adhesive with their eyes very much on the incentive payment, only to find they actually enjoyed the discussion, the exercises and the company of the other participants.

Indeed, there is something about a group setting, the shared anonymity amongst strangers they will never see again, which enables people to gain almost therapeutic benefit from some discussions, about sensitive or embarrassing problems. We have had people tell us that they told the group about an incontinence problem that they had discussed with nobody else – not even their partner or doctor – and others who said they had been inspired to solve personal problems or seek the help they were entitled to as a result. Others clearly regret the briefness of the time together and the anonymity involved.

No, we cannot send you the phone number of the cute guy you sat opposite, or the researcher's personal email – we will gladly forward any additional thoughts or ideas you have after the events that you would like to share with them though (we do ask this when we send our thank-you emails, and people occasionally actually do have brilliant flashes of insight about the research itself on their way home from the group or the next morning that are a pleasure to send on afterwards) but we have often joked in the office that we could make a great side-line operating a dating agency, skilled as we are in categorising people according to their attitudes and behaviours, and the odd bizarre feedback question does tend to bear this out.

Here is a selection of comments received from participants recruited recently, for a range of projects, both qualitative research and user experience:

> *"I didn't really know what to expect to be honest, but I enjoyed it a lot – the money I got was like a bonus after that."*

> *"Honestly I had no idea where they were going with some of the questions they asked me, but they were so nice about it, I really hope what I said is going to be helpful somehow."*

> *"I felt quite tired when I left the building afterwards, and I realised I had been concentrating hard – I think I felt a lot of pressure when I was asked to do things on the website, especially when I couldn't find the feedback form or the social media buttons. I didn't want the lovely researcher to think his site was difficult to use for someone like me, and he was very nice about it, perhaps they will be able to use what I said to make things clearer."*

"My daughter recommended me for this interview because you needed older ladies, and help. The interviewer was a very charming man and I found it easy to talk to even about personal things like my pension. Thank you for inviting me."

"My friends didn't believe I was actually going to get paid for playing computer games, and at last it made me start to wonder if I was getting tricked somehow. But it was me laughing next day and showing them the money, telling them I had a brilliant time – they've all signed up with Saros now and want to take part themselves!"

"Two hours talking about make-up and perfume, it was just like a girls' night in with me mates – well okay there was less alcohol but we did get some cash instead!"

"I was almost disappointed when it finished, as it was such fun talking about my favourite gadgets with a bunch of people as geeky as I clearly am."

"I have been a gaming freak all my life, so to even get to visit the [client's] test lab was brilliant, never mind to get a chance to play an unreleased version of [popular console game title]. I felt like I was meeting celebrities, these were the guys who actually design and test some of my favourite games in the world! I even talked to them about the possibility of interning or doing more stuff for them one day."

"I was a bit nervous as I have never done anything like this before but the people at the research place were so nice... Really welcoming and reassuring. In the end the time went by much quicker than I expected"

"After the focus group I realised I was looking at shopping and how I choose things in a new light, because so much of it I usually do without thinking,

especially the stuff we use at home every day – they made us think really hard about it but I enjoyed it"

"I had applied to take part in so many Saros projects over the years, in fact I nearly unsubscribed, but when I finally got the call was like winning the lottery! The actual interview was quite nice too"

"I enjoyed doing the survey although I had a little difficulty finding the building initially. I am not very technical and was struggling just signing in at reception (rather embarrassingly, but perhaps just nerves) but the guy on reception was very helpful as was the person who conducted the survey who made me feel quite relaxed. The building/offices were certainly interesting and modern".

"As I was discussing a subject which I am particularly enthusiastic about, I kept thinking I was perhaps talking a little too much at times but was happy to give my opinions, answer any questions and perform any tasks expected of me. (I tried to not look at myself on a big screen which was in front of me - aargh!)".

"Thanks for selecting me for this market research project and I was glad to be of assistance and hope I can help again in the future."

"The process was very easy and it was really helpful to receive several reminders. The whole thing was very enjoyable it was really enthusiastic group and we love the product, can't wait for it to come out!"

"It felt like they really cared about what I thought, what my ideas were of which I preferred... Usually no one listens to a word I say."

"Just want to say thank you for an amazing opportunity. The visit to the [brand] office itself was

an experience, what I'd give to work in such a stimulating environment, but the session, getting a chance to preview and, albeit a minuscule part, having input in the creation of something so exciting was fascinating"

"The discussion I took part in was weeks ago, but today I finally saw the ad we help to design I actually feel beyond excited to see it on the TV thank you Saros for getting me involved even though my friends now think I am nuts!"

Conclusions

By sharing feedback at the end of a collaborative and cooperative recruitment project, you as the recruitment purchaser are investing in the continual improvement of our database for the future.

Improving our database also improves the service we can offer you, and means we can continue to attract excellent participants for the future

Sharing your feedback about how your project is managed and administered also helps us to learn and deepen our understanding of your needs next time. Whilst we welcome the challenge of working on any one off or unusual project, it is probably fair to say that we are able to do our best work for clients with whom we have built up a strong relationship based on knowledge and understanding, for whom we recruit regularly and truly get to know their explicit and implicit needs.

We intend to continue innovating in both our project management and database development activities, striving to improve and do better at all times – becoming a partner our clients can rely on to help deliver their very best research.

This brings us back full-circle to our opening words,

people who participate in your research truly are the raw ingredients from which you will craft and forge the actionable insight your clients need and deserve. Working together we will get those ingredients right – the correct balanced blend of premium quality inputs, which will produce a finished product of the utmost quality.

Index

Acknowledgements

This book is about the way a service is delivered, and as such it reflects the efforts and experiences of a lot of people, without whom it would not exist. Any factual errors remain entirely my responsibility, but there are many people I am grateful to for helping bring this publication into existence.

Firstly, my business partner Fiona Jack from Green Light Research – one of many qualitative researchers who knew things needed to change in participant recruitment, but the only one who was ready to invest in making things better. Without that support and involvement Saros would not exist today.

The Saros service to our clients is now delivered by a fantastic team of people, who do the challenging work of getting hundreds of participants selected, recruited, screened and confirmed into events all over the UK every week.

We're lucky enough to have a brilliant team of research bookers, project managers and administrators making it all come together, but particular thanks go to the current Senior Project Management team: Leanne Strick, Darren Strick, Shelley Hodgson, Sarah Spencer and Kate Baker, who work together to make the Saros promise come true for their clients on a consistent and impeccable basis.

As part of the flexible Saros organisation we also depend upon the support of Julia from Ross Franklin, Giles from Blend-Systems, Diana from Social Butterfly and many others, for their specialist business services every day. Gaile from U P Publications has been a pleasure to add to this wider network as we worked towards publication.

Personally, of course, my thanks are due to Richard and my immediate family for encouragement and support, as well as the wider writing and content creation community who have encouraged me to pull this book together, from WABAS to the New Ideas crew.

And when it comes to the wider community, it's important to recognise the role of two other important groups of people... The first are the clients we recruit for. We're lucky to be in a business which is all about enquiry and exploration and being open to new ideas, but it still takes courage to support newer methodologies, and it also takes professional pride to invest in the whole process. We respect and appreciate the people who partner with us to help deliver their insight skills to their clients.

And finally of course, I must thank the many thousands of research participants we have placed in an incredible range of projects since our inception in 2000. From focus groups to eye tracking to food tasting and every conceivable methodology in between, our work depends upon the flexibility, ideas and commitment of this brilliant group of people. It's their ideas and contributions which are the building blocks for all that the research industry delivers, and we're proud to be the point of connection for all that creative communication.

Lightning Source UK Ltd.
Milton Keynes UK
UKOW06f1101040416

271496UK00001B/1/P